Code Like a Girl

Code Like a Girl

Like a Girl

Girl

RAD TECH PROJECTS + PRACTICAL TIPS

MIRIAM PESKOWITZ

ALFRED A. KNOPF · NEW YORK

THIS IS A BORZOI BOOK PUBLISHED BY ALFRED A. KNOPF

Text copyright © 2019 by Miriam Peskowitz
Cover art and interior illustrations copyright © 2019 by Sara Corbett

Grateful acknowledgment is made to the following for permission to
reprint previously published and preexisting materials:

Liz Brown and Jedi Weller: Screenshot of photograph on page 6 used
by permission of Liz Brown and Jedi Weller. All rights reserved.

Fritzing: Images on pages 159, 165 bottom, 170, 171 and 176
created with the Fritzing program used by permission of Fritzing.

The Raspberry Pi Foundation: Images of the Raspberry Pi computer and screenshots
from the Raspberry Pi program used by permission of the Raspberry Pi Foundation.
Raspberry Pi is a trademark of the Raspberry Pi Foundation.

**Scratch, a project of the Scratch Foundation, in collaboration with the Lifelong
Kindergarten Group at the MIT Media Lab:** Screenshots from the Scratch program
used by permission of Scratch, a project of the Scratch Foundation, in collaboration
with the Lifelong Kindergarten Group at the MIT Media Lab.
Scratch is available for free at scratch.mit.edu.

trinket: Screenshots from the trinket.io program by trinket used by
permission of trinket.

Visit us on the Web! rhcbooks.com

Educators and librarians, for a variety of
teaching tools, visit us at RHTeachersLibrarians.com

Library of Congress Cataloging-in-Publication Data
is available upon request.
ISBN 978-1-5247-1389-8 (hc) —
ISBN 978-1-5247-1390-4 (lib. bdg.) —
ISBN 978-1-5247-1391-1 (ebook)

The text of this book is set in 14-point Triplex Serif OT.
The illustrations in the book were created using
Adobe Photoshop and Adobe Illustrator.
Interior design by Sara Corbett.

MANUFACTURED IN CHINA

August 2019
10 9 8 7 6 5 4 3 2 1
First Edition

To Parents and Guardians:

Some projects in this book (particularly in Chapters 4 and 5) involve the use of electronics and tools (such as sewing needles and screwdrivers) that may require your supervision. Please review these chapters before your child begins: you know her best, so please use your own judgment as to how much supervision is required. Please instruct your child on safety basics and please make sure your child reads the following note *before* beginning the book!

Dear Reader,

A few things before you begin reading this book:

In Chapters 4 and 5, you may come across sharp objects that, if not used carefully and with an adult's permission, could be dangerous. We're talking needles, scissors, tin snips, wires, resistors, batteries, conductive thread, copper tape, and/or screwdrivers. As if that weren't enough, there are activities in the book that involve such things as taking apart an old keyboard, pulling the LEDs from a light-up sneaker, and peering inside machines. You definitely want to use out-of-service objects; once we're done, the keyboard, light-up sneaker, machine, etc., may no longer be usable.

So, before doing any of these things, always check first with an adult. To make it easy to know which activities you should be checking in on before starting, the chapters where you should have an adult's permission are marked with a big ⚠ symbol (you can't miss it!).

And, of course—safety first! Here are some basic guidelines to keep in mind (and to keep you and the items in your home safe): never put your fingers or any objects in an outlet and check with an adult before using a plug, never pull a plug out by its cord, and never use electronics when you are near or in water. Don't steal your parents' or anyone else's electronics to use for the projects in this book, and definitely don't take apart any item before first asking an adult's permission. Also, before dismantling your younger sibling's toys and footwear, ask them for permission, too. And while we're at it, don't use email or any social media or programming platform without an adult's permission. Especially if you are a kid. If you're an adult reading this, you can give yourself permission.

I know. Grown-ups. But keep reading. This journey's going to be great!

 LOVE, MIRIAM

TO MY SUPERHEROES:

Meredith, Rob, FJ, Laura, Jean, Angela, Shanise, everyone
else who helped me learn about code, and my mom

Contents

WELCOME

Dear Reader,

Welcome to girl tech world, where we're going to learn some code.

Technology and code are about creativity, self-expression and telling your story. They're about solving problems, being curious, giggling with glee, building things, making the world a better place and creating the future. They're about you: whoever you are, wherever you're at, whatever you want.

Nearly everything you see on a screen is made from code: games, animation, texting, social media, websites, apps, Netflix and the whole entire Internet. *All* of it comes from code, programmed by real people using lots of different coding languages. That's why code is so awesome and powerful.

You see, code is about having an idea and putting it into action. It's about your voice and your vision. From the outside, tech and code may seem puzzling and mysterious, but when you get through the door and past the first few beginner steps and your code starts to work, I tell you, it feels like magic.

When I ask coders and programmers and tech artists why they love what they do, that's exactly what they tell me: it feels like magic. Something didn't exist in the world, and now because of your code, it does. Sure, it's a struggle when your code isn't yet working right, but then, finally, the run works, the app launches, the design sparkles, the electronic music springs to life. You're a creator—you built something—and it's the most amazing feeling in the world.

What's ahead is a journey into tech and code. What's code, really? Directions we use to tell machines what to do. Code comes in different languages, each having its own rules, twists and turns. The good thing? Most languages share the same basic concepts.

FIVE BASIC CONCEPTS

Loops, variables, conditionals, functions, lists (aka arrays). There are more concepts, and they vary across languages, but learn these 5 basics and you can take on anything. I'll point them out as we go along.

We're all beginners here, so I'll let you in on a secret: in tech, the first few steps are the hardest.

Why is that?

Well, first, things will never again be as bewilderingly unfamiliar as they are right now. There are so many new names and concepts, many of which are downright mystifying.

Second, often at the start there's a lot of rigmarole. Signing up. Making new usernames and passwords. Connecting between websites. Downloading programs, not to mention just staring at the screen and wondering what to do next.

Come on in and join our journey. I'll show you the first steps into different types of tech and code, and then point you toward learning more. The Internet is filled with video tutorials, free online coding classes and directions for every language of code, even to program both monsters *and* party dresses from LED lights. It's not so good, though, at providing enough context to get beginners going. That's my job: to get you through the beginning and show you how enchanting all of this is, so the classes and video tutorials will make sense.

I'll also give you a heads-up about where things get hard, so when you experience them, you'll know it's not just you.

What's on the path ahead? Projects and more projects. Games built from the languages Scratch and Python. Animations, podcasts and programs that roll dice and tell stories. We'll poke around a super-secret place called a Terminal, and put together a Raspberry Pi computer; it will have Minecraft built in—so get ready to be creative. We'll take apart electronic toys and gadgets, craft do-it-yourself lanterns and felt bracelets with

LED lights, program LEDs to turn on and off, and turn a picture frame into a glass whiteboard for your room. The finale? A motion detector that sends you an email alert if someone enters your room while you're at school. Really.

We'll build, tinker, hack and code in our own way.

Don't worry if you don't know anything about coding or technology. We'll start with the basics. Push open the doors of a new and vibrant world, where you never know what's coming down the pike. Many of the programmers I met while writing this book told me they taught themselves to code with books and online tutorials. They shared stories about what they learned first, what they gave up on and how they tried again. Some went to college, sure. Others apprenticed with a developer and learned on the job. Many learned with friends. There are endless ways in.

 Welcome aboard. Tech is an amazing journey, and I'm so glad you're here.

Wishing you creativity and confidence and joy.

LOVE, MIRIAM

Q What about social media?

A You and your friends probably have that covered. This book is about how to create and code the next social media platform—or anything else you dream of.

Q Why is it all computer, computer, computer, and not tablets and smartphones?

A Traditionally, programming takes place on computers because they're more powerful. No worries, though. I've searched high and low for ways to code on your phone or tablet and I'll point them out. You can also try to get computer access at the library or your school.

One more thing. If you get confused by anything in the book, reread and try again. If it still doesn't make sense, go to the codelikeagirlbook.com website, where there may be more clues.

P.S. Before we get into the first chapter, I have to show you 2 things.

The first is what a coding team looks like. Meet the Webjunto team. They design apps and help you tell your story through code. I've visited their shop and being there you can't help but want to code and design with them.

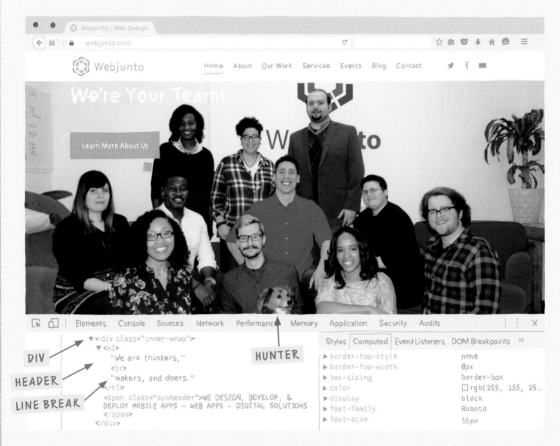

Second, I want to show you the magical see-the-code-behind-a-webpage trick. On the left, notice the brackets filled with letters and numbers, like <div>, <h1> and
? This is the HTML coding language. It provides structure to webpages. Those strange words mean "division," "header1" and "line break." Now look to the right. Do you notice words like *border, box-sizing, color* and *font-family*? These are coded in CSS, a language that gives webpages their style. These 2 languages—HTML and CSS—and a third called JavaScript, work together to create what you can see and do on any screen.

TRY IT!
- - - - - - - -

On a computer, open any webpage and
right-click on it.

    A menu like the one on the right
should pop up. Look for **Inspect** and
click on that. In a flash, the bottom
of the screen should change . . . and
that is code. By clicking on **Inspect**,
you can see the code that's been there
all along, hiding, almost in plain sight.

Back
Forward
Reload
Save As...
Print...
Cast...
Translate to English
View Page Source
Inspect

WHAT DOES RIGHT-CLICK MEAN?

Put the cursor in a website's window. If using a mouse, hold
down the **Control** key on your computer and click on the
mouse's right side. To right-click without a mouse, hold down
the **Control** key and press the right side of the touchpad.
If, on your computer, the **Control** key doesn't work, use the
Command key.

    Uh-oh, mine doesn't work!

    Welcome to technology, where every machine is different
and things don't always work the first time. This is part of the
tech journey.

    First, **Inspect** works on computers, but not on tablets or
phones. If you're at a computer, try it on the Chrome browser.
If right-clicking doesn't work, then, on a PC, try: **Control +
Shift + J**, or **Control + Shift + I**, or the **F12** key. (Don't actually
press the "plus" key—the plus sign means press all keys at
the same time.) On a Mac, try **Command + Alt + I**, or **Command +
Shift + C**.

    But no worries: if none of this works, search online for
"Inspect a website." It's normal if things don't work right
away; tech's middle name is really "troubleshooting."

CHAPTER 1

STARTING TO CODE, WITH SCRATCH

R eady to jump in? Our first destination is Scratch, a programming language that is coded using bright, colorful blocks. Scratch works in your browser, which is the screen window that websites show up on; it's what we use to explore the Internet. Some popular browsers are Chrome, Safari, Firefox and Edge.

Let's do it. On the nearest computer or tablet, open a browser and type in scratch.mit.edu. Hit Enter and you'll find yourself in a brand-new online world. This is Scratch, and it's a space where beginners can create games, animation, art, stories and more—with code.

CODE LIKE A GIRL

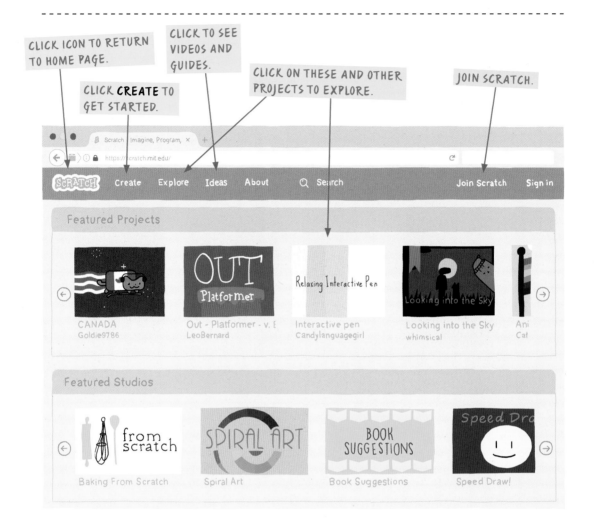

CLICK ICON TO RETURN TO HOME PAGE.

CLICK TO SEE VIDEOS AND GUIDES.

CLICK **CREATE** TO GET STARTED.

CLICK ON THESE AND OTHER PROJECTS TO EXPLORE.

JOIN SCRATCH.

Don't be surprised if your screen's a little different. Software, apps and programs change all the time—and so do screen sizes. Once upon a time, Scratch was only for computers. Now Scratch works on tablets, too. That's great, but we have a word problem. How do we describe pressing a button? I'll use *click*, but if you're coding on a phone or tablet, go on and tap, touch, press, select, drag or pull.

Scratch was created in Boston by the Lifelong Kindergarten group at the MIT Media Lab; MIT stands for Massachusetts Institute of Technology. Don't be misled by the word *Kindergarten* in the title.

Scratch is real programming. Click Create to get started. Now click on a color circle, and you'll see commands that are related to it. These commands are called blocks. To create code, you'll drag and drop the blocks into the workspace. What you can't see is the complex code that makes each block work; that's the genius of Scratch.

I want to tell you something up front. A tech journey can be straight, winding or zigzaggy. It's predictable and unpredictable, and in that way, it's much like the rest of life. Whether you detour or go directly to the Create button, whether you read every word of every chapter in order, or sample in and out, you'll get where you need to be, and at a pace that's right for you. In the tech journey that you're about to embark upon, trust yourself and your curiosity.

Make an Account on Scratch

It's a good idea to create an account on Scratch so you can save your programs, using the Join Scratch button. Pick a name that isn't the same as your actual name and a password. Write them down in a single place where you can keep all your usernames and passwords. **This may be the most important advice I ever give you: write down your username and password.**

Motion

Looks

Sound

Events

Control

Sensing

Operators

Variables

My Blocks

If you don't have an email address, get permission to use your parent's or teacher's. If you're 13, you can create a free Gmail account (search online for "How do I create a Gmail account"). Be sure to check with a parent or guardian first.

CODE LIKE A GIRL

Click Create and a new window opens. This is where we code!

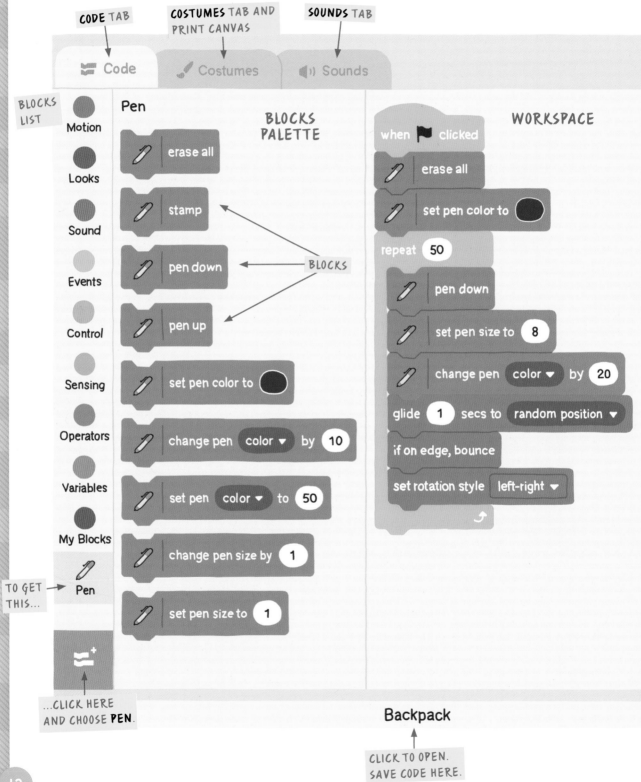

CODE TAB

COSTUMES TAB AND PRINT CANVAS

SOUNDS TAB

≋ Code

🖌 Costumes

🔊 Sounds

BLOCKS LIST

Pen

BLOCKS PALETTE

WORKSPACE

Motion

erase all

when 🚩 clicked

erase all

Looks

stamp

set pen color to ⬤

Sound

pen down

BLOCKS

repeat 50

Events

pen up

pen down

Control

set pen size to 8

Sensing

set pen color to ⬤

change pen color ▾ by 20

Operators

change pen color ▾ by 10

glide 1 secs to random position ▾

if on edge, bounce

Variables

set pen color ▾ to 50

set rotation style left-right ▾

My Blocks

change pen size by 1

Pen

TO GET THIS...

set pen size to 1

...CLICK HERE AND CHOOSE PEN.

Backpack

CLICK TO OPEN. SAVE CODE HERE.

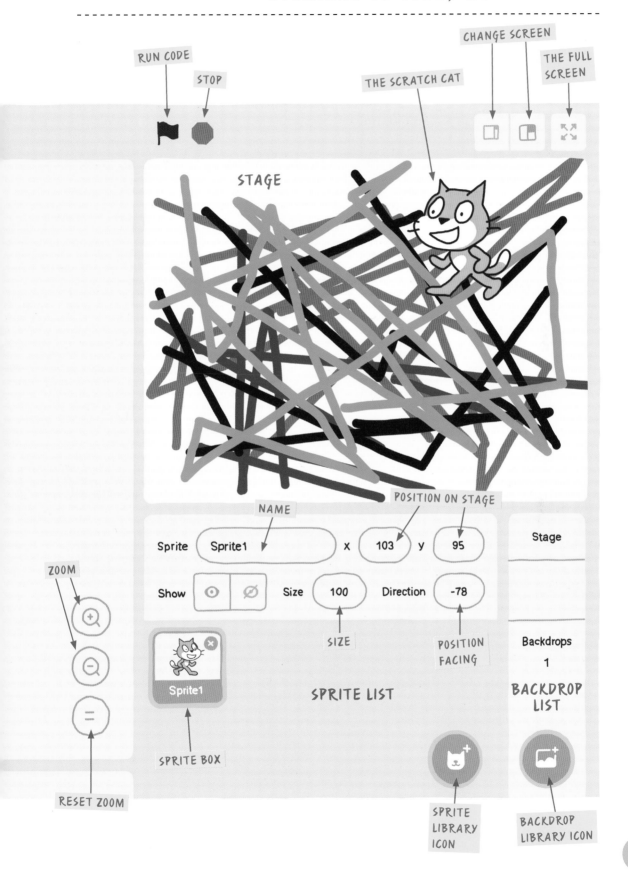

RUN CODE

STOP

CHANGE SCREEN

THE FULL SCREEN

THE SCRATCH CAT

STAGE

POSITION ON STAGE

NAME

Sprite   Sprite1   x   103   y   95   Stage

Show   Size   100   Direction   -78

ZOOM

SIZE

POSITION FACING

Backdrops
1

BACKDROP LIST

Sprite1

SPRITE LIST

RESET ZOOM

SPRITE BOX

SPRITE LIBRARY ICON

BACKDROP LIBRARY ICON

13

CODE LIKE A GIRL

So, now you've signed in and clicked Create. You'll also see a nav bar ("navigation bar") that looks something like this, depending on your device and the size of your screen.

| SCRATCH | ⊕ ▾ | File | Edit | ⚡ Tutorials | Project name | Share | 〟 See Project Page |

When you first find yourself in a new app or platform, take a moment to explore the architecture, which means the way the screens are organized and what happens when you click here and there. Try to understand what's on the screen. Someone, or a team of people, designed and coded the site. Check out the nav bars. Click on the buttons to see where they lead. Right-click on parts of the screen to see if hidden menus pop up. Once you figure out the architecture, this new world will feel much more familiar.

The Stage

The stage is where you'll see, test and run your program. In a new Scratch project, an orange cat will be at center stage. In fact, your very first step will often be to click on the cat's box and then click on the x to make the cat go away. Feel free to do that now.

Sprite1

Backdrops

Below the stage is the Backdrop List. Hover over the Backdrop Library icon and you'll see these options.

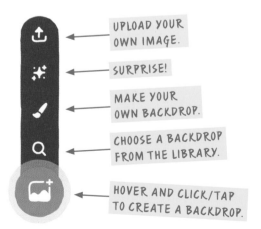

UPLOAD YOUR OWN IMAGE.

SURPRISE!

MAKE YOUR OWN BACKDROP.

CHOOSE A BACKDROP FROM THE LIBRARY.

HOVER AND CLICK/TAP TO CREATE A BACKDROP.

So many choices, but let's start simple, with a make-it-yourself single-color orange backdrop. Hover and

click on the paintbrush, and you'll immediately see the workspace give way as the glories of the paint canvas spring to life. Click Fill and pick a color. Then click on the rectangle tool and make a box that covers the whole canvas by clicking and dragging your mouse in the paint canvas. The color will fill the paint canvas, and you'll see it on the stage, too.

The paint canvas can do quite a lot, so go on and experiment. Click through each of the tools along the side: reshape, brush, line, rectangle, circle. Click the T—for text—to add words and dialogue.

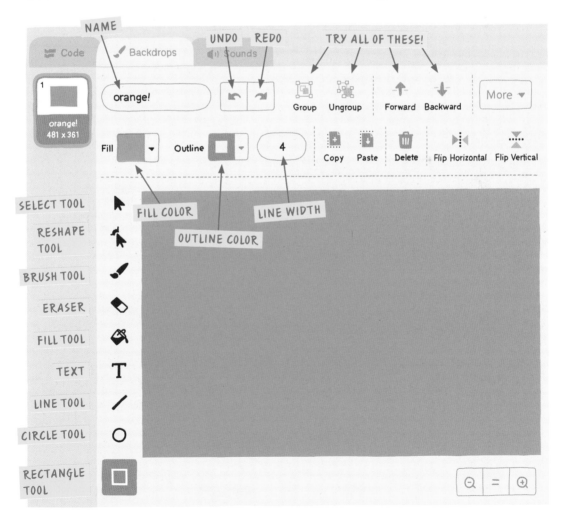

Characters, aka Sprites

Technology is really about telling a story, and that's something we do all the time. Stories need settings—that's why we create backdrops—and they need characters, which is where sprites come in. Why *sprite*? The word comes from animation, and you'll get used to hearing it. A sprite is any image that moves around the screen separately from the backdrop. Lines, letters, people, creatures, monsters, planets—anything can be a sprite. That's because we're creating more than an image. Each individual sprite is programmed, and this code determines what the sprite does, separate from any other character, element or backdrop.

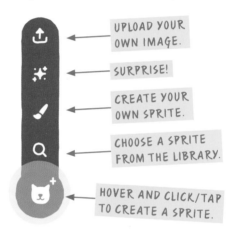

UPLOAD YOUR OWN IMAGE.

SURPRISE!

CREATE YOUR OWN SPRITE.

CHOOSE A SPRITE FROM THE LIBRARY.

HOVER AND CLICK/TAP TO CREATE A SPRITE.

Where do you make sprites? The sprite icon is under the stage, next to the backdrop box. To create a new sprite, do what you did with backdrops: hover over the Sprite Library icon and click to choose or make a sprite. When your sprite makes you smile or helps you imagine a story to tell, you're ready. I picked Blue Dog aka Dog2 from Scratch's Sprite Library because my dog makes me laugh. Once you pick a sprite, you'll see it on the stage.

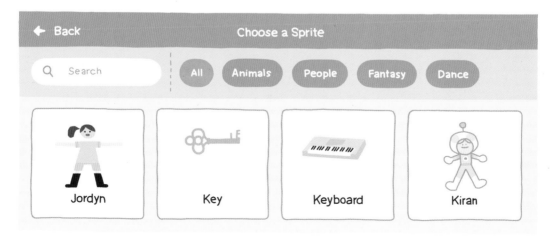

Choose from the Sprite Library and click OK. You'll see your new sprite on the stage.

A program can have many sprites, coded to do different things.

Your new sprite should also show up in the Sprite List below the stage. Click on it and a blue outline will appear. When you have several sprites, this blue outline shows you which sprite is active, so you know which one you are coding.

CODE WITH FRIENDS

The stereotype of coding is that you do it alone. You *can* code by yourself, but coding is also about friendship, teams and community. Bring different people together, and watch a project take off. On the Scratch website,  Scratchers share their projects, have conversations and give each other advice. There's an active community of builders. How big? Around the world, millions of people use Scratch, and most of them are between 10 and 16 years old.

CODE LIKE A GIRL

Where Do We Make the Program?

For us beginners, one of the big mysteries of coding is where it's created. We've checked out the Scratch stage. We created a backdrop and a sprite. Now where do we build the code that makes the sprite come alive?

For each of the projects, first click on the sprite or backdrop box that you want to code. Then follow these general directions:

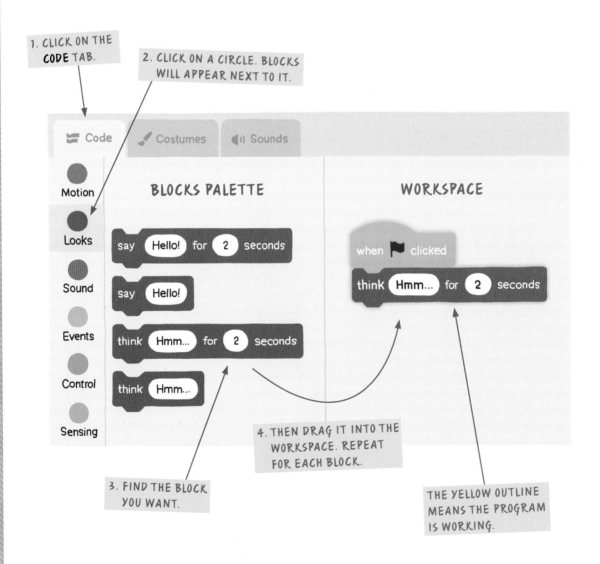

1. CLICK ON THE **CODE** TAB.

2. CLICK ON A CIRCLE. BLOCKS WILL APPEAR NEXT TO IT.

3. FIND THE BLOCK YOU WANT.

4. THEN DRAG IT INTO THE WORKSPACE. REPEAT FOR EACH BLOCK.

THE YELLOW OUTLINE MEANS THE PROGRAM IS WORKING.

Click on one of the colorful circles, and code blocks will appear in the same color, next to it. Like paint on an artist's palette, these blocks are filled with creative possibility. Click on the block you want, then drag and drop it in the workspace, where it will snap together with other blocks. We create code, or scripts, here.

Q Oops, I changed my mind. How do I delete a block?

A Drag it back to the Blocks Palette and watch it disappear! The block doesn't even have to return to its own color. If several blocks are connected, drag one down and the script will break apart.

Hello World!

With Blue Dog and our orange backdrop set, we're ready to code. In a new language, developers write a "Hello World!" program first. It's a big tradition, so that's what we'll do. Follow along on your screen. Find each command in the Blocks Palette and drag and drop it into the workspace.

All Scratch programs begin with an event that gets the action started. The yellow Events circle holds several starter commands. We'll use the when ⚑ clicked command, which means that when someone presses the green flag, the program begins. Okay, that's not rocket science, but you get the idea: every program begins with an event.

STEP 1

Make sure you've clicked into the Blue Dog sprite—its box will have a blue outline—and we're ready to go. Click on the yellow Events circle, and from the Blocks Palette, drag when ⚑ clicked into the workspace.

CODE LIKE A GIRL

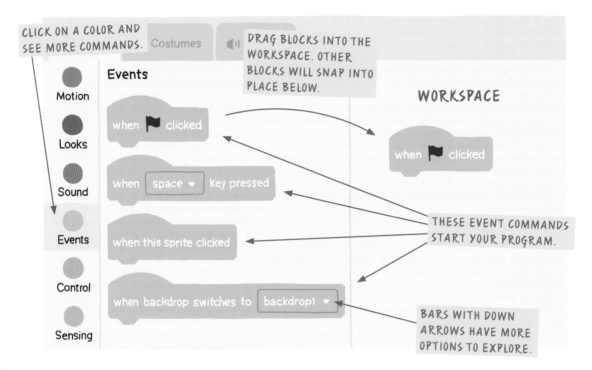

CLICK ON A COLOR AND SEE MORE COMMANDS.

Costumes

DRAG BLOCKS INTO THE WORKSPACE. OTHER BLOCKS WILL SNAP INTO PLACE BELOW.

WORKSPACE

Motion

Looks

Sound

Events

Control

Sensing

Events

when 🚩 clicked

when this sprite clicked

when space ▼ key pressed

when backdrop switches to backdrop1 ▼

when 🚩 clicked

THESE EVENT COMMANDS START YOUR PROGRAM.

BARS WITH DOWN ARROWS HAVE MORE OPTIONS TO EXPLORE.

STEP 2

With the starting event in place, we're ready to code the action. What's the action we want to program? Print Hello World! on the screen. Here's how. Click on the purple circle for Looks, which is a garden of storytelling delight for what sprites can do: Say words and think thoughts. Hide. Switch costumes. Change backdrops. Twirl into new colors, whisk into pixels and whirls, rotate and roll, become ultra-large or super-small.

Find the say Hello! for 2 seconds block. Drag it into the workspace and drop it beneath when 🚩 clicked. It will snap into place.

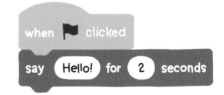

STEP 3

See the white ovals and circles? That means we can replace what's inside. Click into the white space and replace the word Hello! with Hello World!

Change 2 seconds to 10 so Hello World! will stay on-screen longer. In Scratch, any white space can be changed.

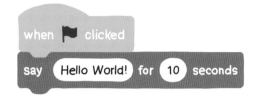

You're almost ready for something amazing to happen.

Click on your sprite and pull it to center stage. Press the green flag, because that's the event we chose to start the program.

Voilà! Hello World!

You did it! You are now the real deal, an official coder and part of its traditions. Hello World! (And welcome to the world of coding.)

I almost forgot something big: save your program. Look for File, click into it and select Save now. Always save programs. (If your program doesn't save, it's probably because you need to join Scratch or sign in.)

Blue Dog's Story

Let's take Blue Dog for a walk. This project creates a story that uses several backdrops and gives Blue Dog a few lines. Sometimes we know the story we're telling. Maybe we've sketched the scenes or made a storyboard. We've had an idea for days and we can't wait to bring it alive. Other times we dive in with a starting place and half a plan, and the story unfolds as we go. All are good. For this story I picked backdrops from the Backdrop Library, where I found our pup a bedroom and 2 outdoor scenes.

Remember where to get backdrops? Beneath the stage, look for the Backdrop Library icon (see page 13).

CODE LIKE A GIRL

Each morning, Blue Dog wakes up and goes running in the woods with her dog friends. Today, though, she walks out her bedroom door and is mysteriously transported to an unfamiliar street in California with a graffiti-filled wall. What's up with that?

What you can't see because this is a book and not a computer screen: Blue Dog is animated and glides smoothly across the room.

"What happened to the hallway?" she may be wondering. "Where's the front door? Where's my person?"

The usual landmarks have disappeared. Then, before Blue Dog can even get used to the new street, everything shifts. She takes in the new setting, a garden, but this is getting weird. Worries fill her mind. "Am I far away? Am I dreaming? How will I get back home to find my dog friends and my person? Should I be excited, or scared?"

It's not Pixar or Disney, true. It is the start of a basic, simple story that can become longer and more layered over time.

So how do we code this? I'll walk you through, step by step.

* To start a new project, click File > New.

* Clear away the cat (click the cat's sprite box and then click on the x).

* Pick a sprite, and then choose 3 backdrops, following the directions above. (I chose Bedroom 2, Mural and Pathway.)

Here's the full script. Remember—to code, click into your sprite and drag these blocks from their color categories onto the workspace, changing the content of the white spaces to match what's here.

BLUE DOG'S STORY

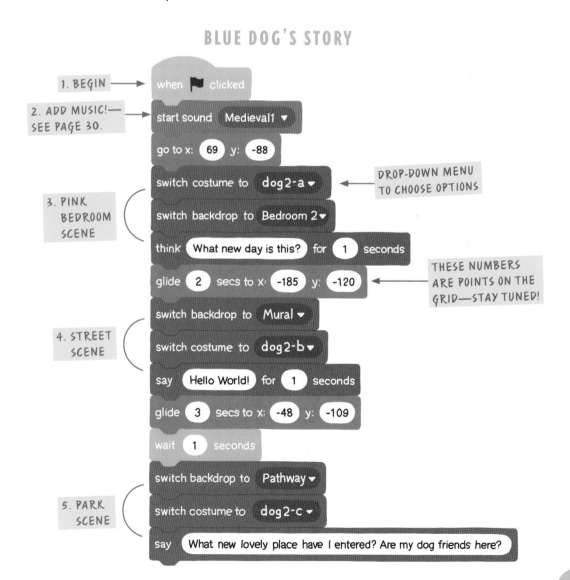

1. BEGIN → when ⚑ clicked

2. ADD MUSIC!— SEE PAGE 30. → start sound Medieval1 ▾

go to x: 69 y: -88

switch costume to dog2-a ▾ ← DROP-DOWN MENU TO CHOOSE OPTIONS

3. PINK BEDROOM SCENE

switch backdrop to Bedroom 2 ▾

think What new day is this? for 1 seconds

glide 2 secs to x: -185 y: -120 ← THESE NUMBERS ARE POINTS ON THE GRID—STAY TUNED!

switch backdrop to Mural ▾

4. STREET SCENE

switch costume to dog2-b ▾

say Hello World! for 1 seconds

glide 3 secs to x: -48 y: -109

wait 1 seconds

switch backdrop to Pathway ▾

5. PARK SCENE

switch costume to dog2-c ▾

say What new lovely place have I entered? Are my dog friends here?

CODE LIKE A GIRL

Your code is in the workspace, but what's going on?

1 **The story begins.** The starting event is when 🚩 clicked.

2 **Add a soundtrack.** Use the start sound block from the magenta Sound circle. I chose a medieval tune from the Sound Library, and you'll choose whatever appeals to you. (See Sounds! on page 30 for directions.)

3 **Scene one: morning (pink bedroom scene).** Blue Dog wakes, thinks "What new day is this?" and walks to the corner of the room. But wait! She's facing the wrong direction!

THE BLUE DOG FLIP

Click Blue Dog's sprite box, then click the **Costumes** tab. You'll see 3 costumes. Click the first one, dog2-a. Click the **Select** tool ⬐. Click **Flip Horizontal**. Now Blue Dog faces the right direction!

Flip Horizontal   Flip Vertical

WALKING HOW?

Blue Dog walks by "gliding." It takes her 2 seconds to get from the bed to the bottom left corner. Want to speed this up? Change the number. Gliding across the stage in .1 second is swift; going the same distance in 10 seconds is slow motion. And how do you tell Blue Dog where to stop? That brings us to the grid!

THE GRID!

Because computers are more precise than we humans are, we can't just say, "Hey, Blue Dog, start a little bit left of center—no, maybe an inch higher—and go to the left. Yeah, that looks good, but stretch a little bit toward the top. Thanks."

Instead, we use the x coordinate and y coordinate to tell Blue Dog where to walk.

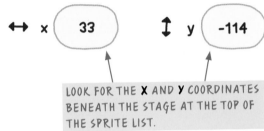

LOOK FOR THE X AND Y COORDINATES BENEATH THE STAGE AT THE TOP OF THE SPRITE LIST.

The numbers help you code:

* Every spot on the grid can be named with an x and y pair of numbers.

* The center of the stage's grid is x=0 and y=0.

* The horizontal line is the x axis. Its range is −240 to 240.

y= 180

x= -240   0,0   x= 240

y= -180

* The vertical line is the y axis, and its range is −180 to 180.

Some of you like math, and for you this may make sense right away. Some of you are less math-y, but trust me, over time the grid will feel more familiar. Move your sprite in all directions and watch the numbers change.

Send a Card to a Friend

Q My friend is sad because she didn't make the basketball travel team (and her friend did). I want to make a card that tells her that she's awesome and it's all going to be okay. Can you help?

A Definitely. Let's make a digital card with some inspirational sayings. Even if right now she's angry and sad that she didn't make the team and her friend did, being disappointed is okay; everyone feels like that from time to time and life has fantastic things ahead for her.

How do we make this card? Well, coding is a thought process. It's translation. We take a vision, break it down into small steps, put those small steps in order and build them with code.

The next page shows one way to do it. On the left is the vision, in small steps. On the right is our plan.

Q Is there only one way to code this?

A No, and that's the beauty of coding. There are often many, many ways to build something from code.

Hey, Rosa!
We know you're down, but...

Love Yourself Always.

Dream Big.

You got this!

We love you, and you're an awesome friend.

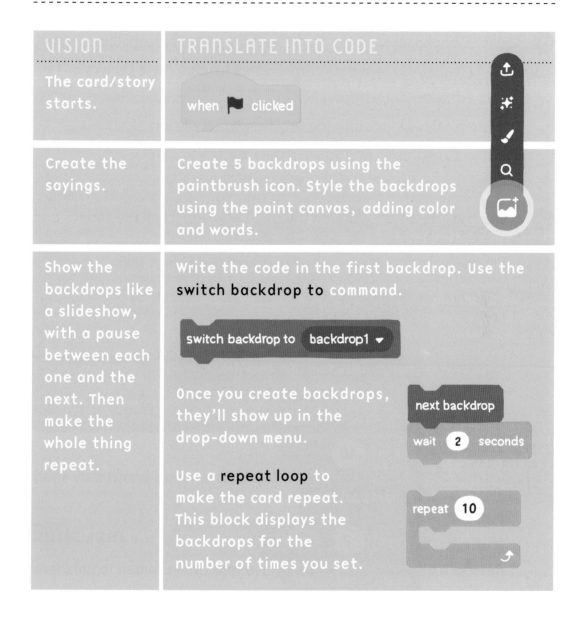

VISION	TRANSLATE INTO CODE
The card/story starts.	when 🏴 clicked
Create the sayings.	Create 5 backdrops using the paintbrush icon. Style the backdrops using the paint canvas, adding color and words.
Show the backdrops like a slideshow, with a pause between each one and the next. Then make the whole thing repeat.	Write the code in the first backdrop. Use the **switch backdrop to** command. switch backdrop to backdrop1 ▾ Once you create backdrops, they'll show up in the drop-down menu. next backdrop wait 2 seconds Use a **repeat loop** to make the card repeat. This block displays the backdrops for the number of times you set. repeat 10

> The more familiar you become with a programming language, the easier it is to "think" in that language.

Now that we've sketched out our plan, let's code. Create a new Scratch window (File › New), click the cat's sprite box and click the x to clear the stage. Let's get your friend feeling better.

1 Choose a backdrop.

2 Choose 3 letter sprites from the Sprite Library › Letters, or make them yourself with the paint option.

3 To code, we will use the magenta Sound blocks to add a sound effect to each of the 3 letter sprites—and link the effects to keys we can play on our keyboard.

What happens next? That thought process for making a vision real: we'll start calling it The Formula, and we can use it to create code for any program we can imagine! Here's The Formula for JAM: it uses 3 different ways to make music and link the music to a sprite. Let's code.

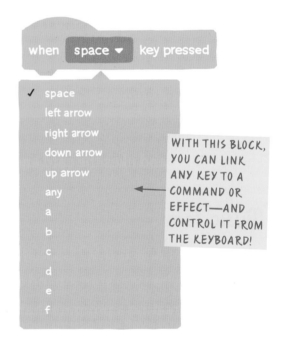

WITH THIS BLOCK, YOU CAN LINK ANY KEY TO A COMMAND OR EFFECT—AND CONTROL IT FROM THE KEYBOARD!

OUR VISION	MAKE IT HAPPEN!
J creates a musical background.	Click on the J sprite box to start to code. See the blue outline? That means you're in J.

In the yellow **Events** circle, start the action with **when this sprite clicked**. This means to get the music started, you'll actually click or tap the J sprite.

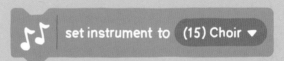

Next we code the **Music** blocks, but where are they?

1 Look toward the bottom of the Blocks List and click this button:

2 On the page that opens, choose **Music**.

3 Now on the Blocks List, you should see the music notes! Click to see the green **Music** blocks.

Use the green **set instrument to** block. Press the down arrow to pick from cello, electric guitar, piano, bassoon and more. I chose 15, a choir.

🎵🎵 set instrument to (15) Choir ▼

Use the green **play note** block. In the white space, choose your note. I chose 62, which is a D. Set the length: 60 beats keeps the sound going for a while.

When done, the script will look like this:

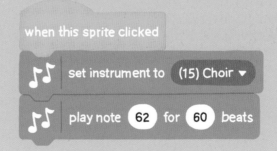

A is a snare drum beat, played with the left arrow key.

Click the A sprite box. The workspace should be empty.

Start the action with the **when space key pressed** block; click on the down arrow and choose **left arrow**.

Use the green **play drum** block. There are 18 types of percussion instruments, including bass drum, snare drum, 3 cymbals, tambourine, hand clap, cowbell, bongo, conga and more. Choose #1, the snare drum (or any drum you want). Click into the white window and set it for .05 beats.

M is a beatbox loop, played with the space bar.

Click on the M sprite box. Pull out the **when space key pressed** block. We can play the sound with the space bar.

when space ▼ key pressed
start sound Human Beatbox1 ▼

1 To get the beatbox: click into the **Sounds** tab, click on the Sound Library icon and select **Human Beatbox 1**. Pick it, then click the **Code** tab.

CHOOSE A SOUND.

SOUND LIBRARY

2 From the magenta **Sound** circle, pull out **start sound**. Click the down arrow to find the beatbox. This links the sound to the code.

Human Be...

You got it. The 3 scripts will look like this.

When you're ready to play, drag the letter sprites to where you want them on stage. Play music with the left arrow, the space bar, and by clicking or tapping the J sprite, just like your code says.

Take it from here. Add more sound-sprite combos. Change the colors, add special effects, make the letters move, bounce, spin. Enjoy!

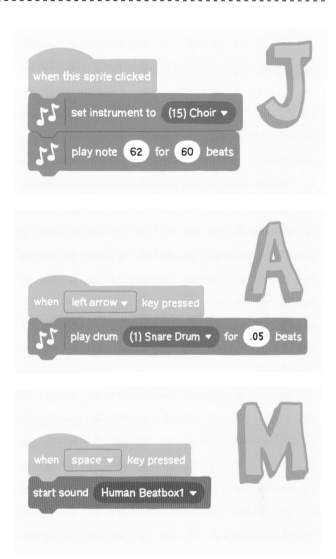

Q It looks messy, the scripts are on different screens and I can't see all 3 at the same time. Will this work?

A Yes. You'll see only one sprite's code at a time, but Scratch can see and run all the code.

Your Story Matters, or How to Podcast in Scratch

A podcast is a recorded story or report, or anything, in your voice. This is all the code it takes to podcast on Scratch.

BASIC PODCAST CODE

The code is the simple part. Knowing your story and saying it out loud? Maybe that comes easily to you, and I hope it does. If you ever feel like you have nothing important to say, or that your story doesn't matter, then this is for you. The world needs to hear your voice. We're better off when we hear everyone's story, and that definitely includes yours. You matter, and you have many interesting or funny or important or poignant things to express. Just because you're you.

Record Your Podcast!

1. Create a sprite and add the 2 blocks of code shown above.

2. Now, create the content. Click the Sounds tab. Hover over the Sound Library icon and click into Record. The Record Sound box opens. Press Record and start telling us what you think.

3   When you're done, press Stop Recording. Save (or re-record). Name it, and polish things up with Trim and other editing tools.

4   Click on the Code tab. In the magenta play sound until done block, click the down arrow and choose your recording. This is Scratch's behind-the-scenes way of attaching the recording to your code.

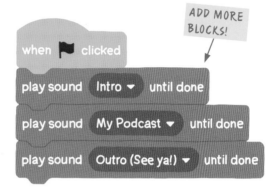

ADD MORE BLOCKS!

when 🏳 clicked

play sound   Intro ▾   until done

play sound   My Podcast ▾   until done

play sound   Outro (See ya!) ▾   until done

For an extra challenge: use the Sounds tab to create a musical intro for the beginning and a spoken outro for the end (like "Goodbye for now, see you next week").

Beach Balls

This animation can be used by itself or as part of a Scratch story or game. Some animators create different sprite costumes and use code to play them together, fast. We'll use the costume feature to create 3 versions of a beach ball and code some blocks to make all the balls change and move.

Start with 1 beach-ball sprite from the Sprite Library (or make your own, of course). Click the Costumes tab. Right-click or tap the beach-ball box for the inner menu and press duplicate. Do this again. You'll end up with 3 costumes of a single beach-ball sprite. Click into each costume and style it using the paint canvas.

SPRITE COSTUMES

Beachball

Beachball 2

Beachball 3

CODE LIKE A GIRL

You're probably getting the rhythm of this: pop in a starting event, like when 🏳 clicked. To create the animation, follow these steps:

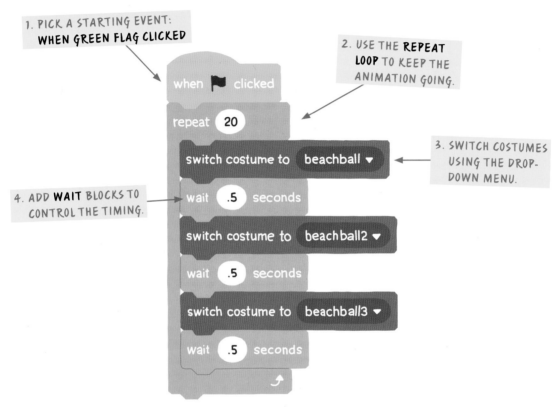

1. PICK A STARTING EVENT: **WHEN GREEN FLAG CLICKED**

2. USE THE **REPEAT LOOP** TO KEEP THE ANIMATION GOING.

3. SWITCH COSTUMES USING THE DROP-DOWN MENU.

4. ADD **WAIT** BLOCKS TO CONTROL THE TIMING.

Go on—click the green flag and run your animation!

DRY Your Code

See how the switch costume and wait blocks repeat a few times? Code likes to be elegant and concise so it can run faster. There's a coding concept called DRY—don't repeat yourself. Let's "refactor" our beach-ball program. That means changing some code, but not changing what the program does.

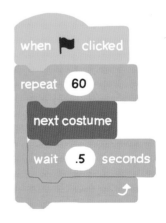

Try running it. This code does the same job as the first, but uses fewer lines. That's DRY. Now we could add 100 costume changes, and run all of them with this little bit of code.

Got it working? Add this second script to get the beach ball moving.

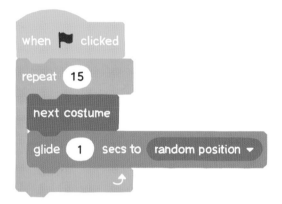

Now try this:

What's ahead? We're going to build a game. It will take many steps, and that's normal. When I was learning my first programs, I was astounded that they took so many lines. This is how coding goes, and when we're done, you'll have a full working game to play.

City Lights Game

Dear Reader,

You've got to know about remix. By now you've probably stashed several programs in your personal Scratch studio, and you may have realized you can look inside everyone else's Scratch projects, too. If not, let me tell you Scratch's big secret: remix. On the Scratch home page, follow the Explore button, and click into a project that intrigues you. Click See Inside to check out their code. Like it? Click Remix. You'll end up with a copy that's yours to play with and change.

The Remix button creates a brand-new copy of someone else's code and saves it for you. The original program stays as it was, and you can now tinker with yours any way you like.

"That must be cheating!" you gasp.

No. In the world of tech, remix is not cheating. It's a legit and common practice. There are open source repos, or repositories, of code online, where people store their code for others to see. (Instead of remix, they call it "forking.") True, this doesn't usually happen at companies, which often keep their code secret so their competitors don't steal it. In the Scratch community, it's considered an honor when people remix your project. Just make sure you give credit. Like this: "The game we're about to make—City Lights—is a creative remix of Scratch's 'Hide and Seek.' Thanks for your generous spirit, Scratch."

 LOVE, MIRIAM

Designing City Lights

City Lights is a game with 3 space creatures named Tera, Giga and Pico. (You can find them in the Scratch Sprite Library.) In the game, the space creatures appear and disappear, and you score points by clicking on them. To build the game, first we'll create and style the sprites; then we'll program the code. So settle in—we'll be at this for a while.

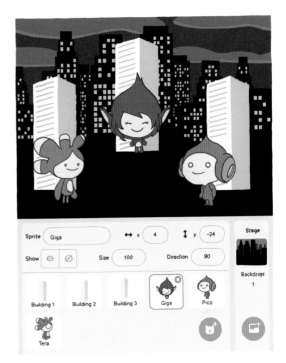

STEP 1

Let's open Scratch (scratch.mit.edu). On the home page, click Create. Prepare the stage by making the orange cat disappear. (Remember? In the Sprite List, click the cat's box so the blue outline appears, then click x. That cat should scat.)

STEP 2

Pick a backdrop. Hover over and click into the Backdrop Library and choose Outdoors › Night City (under the Outdoors button). After you choose the backdrop, you should see it in the Backdrop List, and it should fill the stage.

The Formula for the Forever Loop

WHAT DO WE WANT TO DO?	WHAT CODE MAKES THIS HAPPEN?
Move Tera to Building 1.	Click on the blue **Motion** circle and pull out the **go to random position** block. `go to random position ▼` Click the down arrow—the menu should include the names of all the sprites you created. Pick **Building 1**. `go to Building 1 ▼` This will send Tera to Building 1.
Tera hides behind Building 1.	From the purple **Looks** circle, drag and drop the **hide** block. `hide`
Tera continues to hide. We have to ask another question: How long should she wait before showing herself?	Use the **wait** block from the orange **Control** circle. `wait 1 seconds` It's no fun if Tera is predictable. Let's make her hide and show up randomly. `DRAG HERE` `pick random 1 to 10` Click in the green **Operators** circle, find the **pick random** block and drag it into the **wait** block. The small white space will expand to hold it, I promise. `wait pick random 1 to 6 seconds` Change the numbers to 1 and 6. This will pick a random number between 1 and 6. That's how many seconds Tera will hide.

This is a big deal: you're programming randomizers!

Tera should move to a random place on the stage, but not too far from her building.

That randomizer trick? We're going to do it again to control how far Tera moves. From the blue **Motion** circle, pull out the **move 10 steps** command.

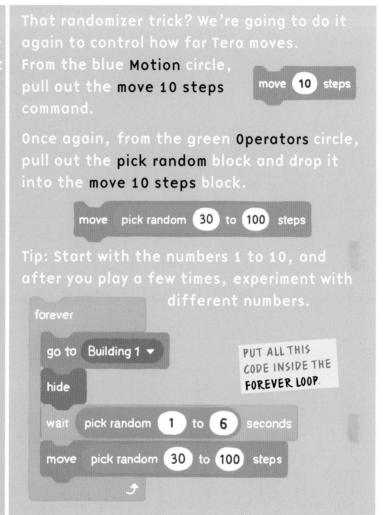

Once again, from the green **Operators** circle, pull out the **pick random** block and drop it into the **move 10 steps** block.

Tip: Start with the numbers 1 to 10, and after you play a few times, experiment with different numbers.

PUT ALL THIS CODE INSIDE THE FOREVER LOOP.

Wait, remember the **hide** block? We haven't shut it off yet, which means that even though Tera has moved away from the building, she's still invisible.

Solution: Make Tera visible so the player can click on her. From the purple **Looks** circle, drag and drop the **show** block to beneath the **move pick random 30 to 100 steps** block.

And one more thing:

We want Tera to stay on-screen for a little bit so the player has a chance to click on her and score.	From the orange **Control** circle, drag and drop the **wait** block to just below the **show** block.	

Because these lines of code are tucked inside the forever loop, the sequence will continue endlessly (or until someone clicks the red Stop button).

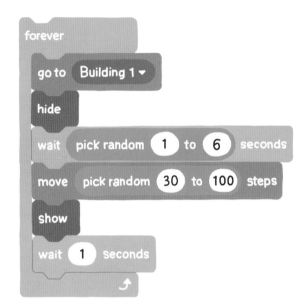

Coding is about making decisions. A question like "How many seconds should Tera wait?" is really about how hard the game should be, right? It's up to us to decide. A one-second wait makes for a very fast game, but try it out and see. If it's too hard to catch and click on the sprites, increase the wait time so they stay visible for longer. Try different numbers, or use the randomizer.

Are We *Still* Coding This Game?

Yes, but we're almost done with Tera. Let's start the second script, or section of code. Our goal when a player clicks on Tera: the score changes, and we see a surprise special effect—Tera changes color.

Pull over these 3 blocks. Try out different numbers to change the effect.

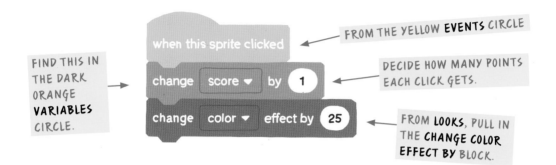

FROM THE YELLOW **EVENTS** CIRCLE

FIND THIS IN THE DARK ORANGE **VARIABLES** CIRCLE.

DECIDE HOW MANY POINTS EACH CLICK GETS.

FROM **LOOKS**, PULL IN THE **CHANGE COLOR EFFECT BY** BLOCK.

The Backpack

Congrats! You're done with Tera's code. Hit that Save Now button! That was a lot of work, so let's reuse it. I mean, if it's okay to copy another coder's work, you can definitely copy your own! Developers reuse their code all the time rather than retype the lines. We can use most of Tera's code for the 2 other space creatures. How? Just below the workspace is the Backpack. To open, click or tap on it. Pull each script inside.

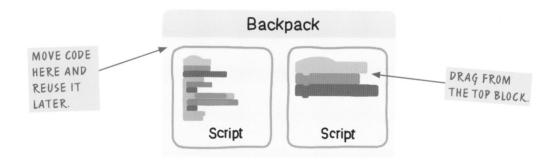

MOVE CODE HERE AND REUSE IT LATER.

DRAG FROM THE TOP BLOCK.

When that's done, get ready to code the other 2 space creatures, reusing our own code.

It's Giga's Turn!

We know that in Scratch, each sprite has its own code. To program the other 2 space creatures, we'll reuse Tera's code but change a few details.

Click on Giga's sprite box. Her workspace is empty. Go to Backpack and drag the 2 scripts into the workspace. Tip: Drag from the top and the blocks should stick together.

1 Let's change the code so that Giga hides behind Building 2. Use the drop-down menu to do this.

2 Let's give Giga her own special effect. Delete the change color effect by block, and add the play sound until done block from the magenta Sound circle. When clicked, Giga will play music.

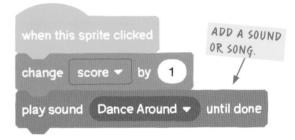

ADD A SOUND OR SONG.

Remember how to program sound (page 30)? Click into the **Sounds Tab > Sound Library > Loops > Dance Around**. Choose this loop and it will show up in the **play sound until done** block's pull-down menu.

That's it for Giga. See, coding does get easier.

Now Pico

Click on Pico's box and click on the Code tab. Same deal: drag the 2 scripts from the Backpack into Pico's workspace.

We'll make the same changes.

1 In the drop-down menu for the blue go to block, pick Building 3.

2 What happens when Pico is caught? How about if Pico says "Hello!" and sprinkles fairy dust? (And of course, you can type in something way more interesting!)

ADD A FAIRYDUST SOUND AND SAY HELLO!

The Buildings Need Code, Too: Layers

It may look like the buildings don't need any code, but they do. The space creatures have to hide, which means that when the game starts, the 3 buildings need to move to the front layer of the stage—so the space creatures can be behind them.

This is totally normal: graphics and animations have layers, and we use code for that. A bird flies across a stand of trees. If we want the bird to fly in front of the trees, we move the bird to the front layer. If we want the bird to fly behind the trees, we code the bird into a back layer. If we want more complex action, we

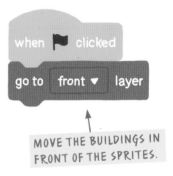

MOVE THE BUILDINGS IN FRONT OF THE SPRITES.

can code the bird to weave in and out, flying in front of some trees and behind others. (When you get the game set up, remove the go to front layer block so you can see what difference it makes.)

Of course, once you add this code to the first building, reuse it. Pop the script into the Backpack, click into each of the other 2 buildings, and pull the script into their workspace.

City Lights Is Ready to Play

Wow, you did it! After all that work, you built a full game. Enjoy it. Send it to your friends—directions for sharing a Scratch project are back on page 35. When you're ready, iterate and change it up. Make buildings smaller or larger. Use different characters, and make some harder to catch—you can score more points when you click them. Add a timer so that the game stops after 2 minutes, or set up a system so that when the score reaches 20, the game turns into a new level with a new backdrop. It's your vision and your game.

> To feel comfy in Scratch or any language, try to do some coding every day, just like practicing an instrument or sport.

Wait, I Want More Scratch!

1 Try the tutorials you find on Scratch.

2 Explore Scratch projects. Remix them to figure out how they work.

3 Set up a game to write some code using each Scratch block—it's a great way to journey through all of Scratch. Search online for "Scratch Wiki Blocks" for a guide to each one.

4 Make your own ideas! When you have a vision, sketch a box with The Formula, just like we've been doing, and translate your vision into code. It will happen, little by little, and you'll start to feel the magic.

Dear Reader,

We've been on quite a journey. Turn back to the first few pages of the book, and you'll see how far we've come from our first Hello World! program. Right about now is the time to talk about perfectionism, which many girls (and boys and grown adults, too) suffer from. It can come up big-time when coding, because we want everything to be right immediately, and yet when we're coding, something always seems to go wrong.

Perfectionism sounds great, but it isn't. Perfectionists set impossible and unattainable goals. When these goals can't be reached, perfectionists feel like unworthy failures. It's terrible for them when that happens. It feels so bad that they may stop trying a new thing unless they think they have it nailed.

These are perfectionist voices: "If I can't get it right the first time, I won't try." "This is taking too long, so I must not be any good at it." "Someone's keeping score on me." "I can't make mistakes."

Some people start coding, get a few steps in and then quit. It's unfamiliar and weird. If this feels like it might be you, don't quit. Not yet.

Why?

Because this frustration is normal. Coding is all about trial and error, remixing and debugging. It's about experimenting and change. Coding is about checking out new possibilities just because you feel like it, and maybe this time it will work. It's about troubleshooting to find out why it didn't work! To code is to recognize that despite our dearest dreams and best intentions, anything can go awry at any time. It's just the way life is. Code is a ton of details put all in the right order to turn an idea into an app, or a game, or whatever. And we get there one small step at a time.

This is what makes coding the absolutely most extraordinary solution to perfectionism ever. It's like they're made for each other.

Coding is a fantastic way to realize that mistakes are not nearly as bad as they seem, that they can be found and fixed, no big deal. If you stick with code, you can build things, do what you love, make your voice heard, earn money and contribute to the world around you.

In the next chapter, we'll step away from code for a moment, because we're going to put together a computer. Really. You'll meet my friend Meredith. She recently moved to New York, though we still text and phone all the time and visit each other when we can. She's one of my favorite people to talk tech with.

 LOVE, MIRIAM

CHAPTER 2

MAKE YOUR OWN COMPUTER WITH RASPBERRY PI

Dear Reader,

My friend Meredith showed me the awesome Raspberry Pi box. We were sitting at the breakfast bar in her apartment. "Don't be fooled by the delectable raspberry logo," she said, pointing to the picture on the box's label. She opened the box and unwrapped a palm-sized machine. "This is fantastic. It's a $35 computer, and it comes preloaded with Minecraft and Scratch and a bunch of other things. It's a little hard to put together, but it's an actual, real computer when you're done." I put on my game face. "OMG," I thought. "She's a Harvard computer science

graduate who built her first computer when she was 11. If it's hard for her, what are *my* chances?"

Not that that's a reason to give up.

The Raspberry Pi computer is tiny, and it does fit in the palm of your hand. To make it into a usable desktop computer, we attach a keyboard and a mouse and connect the Raspberry Pi computer to a screen, which could be a computer monitor or a TV screen. Connect the Pi to an electrical outlet, and you have your own computer to use.

This little computer was created in Britain. The people behind it had 2 dreams: they wanted a computer that was affordable, so everyone could have one, and they wanted more of us to understand what happens inside a computer. As they see it, computers and electronic devices are everywhere, but few of us have any idea how they work. Many of our devices are closed systems, like Xboxes and iPads. That means you can't get "under the hood" and see what's going on inside. With a Raspberry Pi computer, you can see everything. You make the connections. You're in control.

We're going to make a fully working computer. Developers always say things like "Read the documentation," but honestly, often the official directions aren't so clear. The first time I put together a Raspberry Pi computer, I read the laminated directions card, and my brain buzzed with fuzzy words like *NOOBS* and *Raspbian* that meant nothing to me. I had to google everything, and then I got distracted and started to read an ebook, and *then* I decided to go outside and walk my dog.

Tech changes fast. Your Raspberry Pi computer may be older or newer or smaller than this one. It may have extra pins or features! In tech, you learn to roll with new updates.

Like Blue Dog in the first chapter, I'd entered a place that was very unfamiliar. I knew what software was, kind of. But what was this tech in front of me? I figured it out, though, and now I can guide you through the process and explain some things up front.

 LOVE, MIRIAM

Q I don't have a Raspberry Pi computer yet. What should I do?

A Just read along (and make plans to get one!). I'll do my best to make you feel like you're plugging in cords along with us.

CHALLENGE 1

The Raspberry Pi Computer Scavenger Hunt

There's a long tradition of creating a computer from mismatchy parts, so let's start a scavenger hunt to find the parts we need. Our goal: find a keyboard, mouse, screen, power cord, a way to connect to the Internet, and a few other things that will make our new computer work.

Here's our list!

- ☐ **Raspberry Pi computer.** Purchase from raspberrypi.org or an online electronics store like adafruit.com, sparkfun.com or amazon.com.

- ☐ **Keyboard and mouse,** so you can tell the Pi what to do. These are often the easiest parts to find.

- ☐ **Screen,** so you can see what the computer is doing inside. Your screen can be a TV or a computer monitor.

CODE LIKE A GIRL

☐ **HDMI cable,** to connect the Raspberry Pi to the screen. This is the same cable that connects a TV to most gaming consoles. Read ahead to Challenge 2 (page 70) to find the right one.

☐ **Micro SD card.** SD stands for "secure digital." It's the memory. It will save what you do on your new computer, and it holds the operating system. An 8GB micro SD card is fine, but a 16GB is better. This small memory card slips into a slot underneath the Pi. (It's also the kind of memory card used in some cell phones and cameras.) This is the one part that you'll probably have to purchase, and if you do, get the type that comes preloaded with NOOBS—which stands for New Out Of Box Software—and Raspbian, which is Raspberry Pi's operating system.

☐ **Micro USB power cord (5V and 2.5A),** so you can plug the Pi into an electrical outlet. Many but not all cell phone chargers will fit *and* will provide enough power.

☐ **Headphones, earbuds or speakers,** which you'll need if your monitor or screen doesn't have built-in audio.

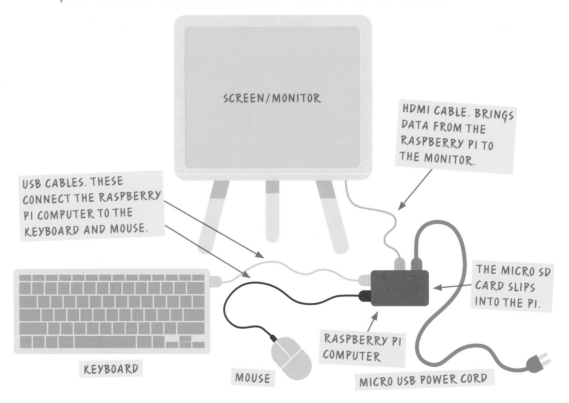

SCREEN/MONITOR

HDMI CABLE. BRINGS DATA FROM THE RASPBERRY PI TO THE MONITOR.

USB CABLES. THESE CONNECT THE RASPBERRY PI COMPUTER TO THE KEYBOARD AND MOUSE.

THE MICRO SD CARD SLIPS INTO THE PI.

RASPBERRY PI COMPUTER

KEYBOARD

MOUSE

MICRO USB POWER CORD

WIFI DONGLE

☐ **Internet connection.** The Raspberry Pi 3 and newer ones have built-in wireless and Bluetooth. An older Pi will need an Ethernet cord or a WiFi *dongle*. (Welcome to weird tech words, and I swear I'm not making this one up. It's a small gadget that pops into a USB port and connects to WiFi.)

☐ **Case.** Purchase one, or build it from LEGOs, wood, a lunch box or any container. Just make sure there's room for the plugs and cables and that air can circulate so your Raspberry Pi computer won't get too hot.

How do we find these parts? That's where the scavenger hunt comes in. Maybe there's a computer lying around that doesn't work, but the monitor and keyboard are still good. Take them, and cross those items off your list. Maybe a cell phone has a power cord that fits. Plug it in, and if it works, that's done. Ask your family and friends. Search yard sales, a neighbor's basement or secondhand shops. Local businesses may have older keyboards, mice and monitors lying around that no one uses anymore, and they may agree to give them to you for free, or sell them to you at very low cost.

NOT A BIG FAN OF SCAVENGER HUNTS?

You *can* purchase a ready-to-go kit with all the parts for your Raspberry Pi. That's the quick, but more expensive, approach. For suggestions, see codelikeagirlbook.com/supplies.

CODE LIKE A GIRL

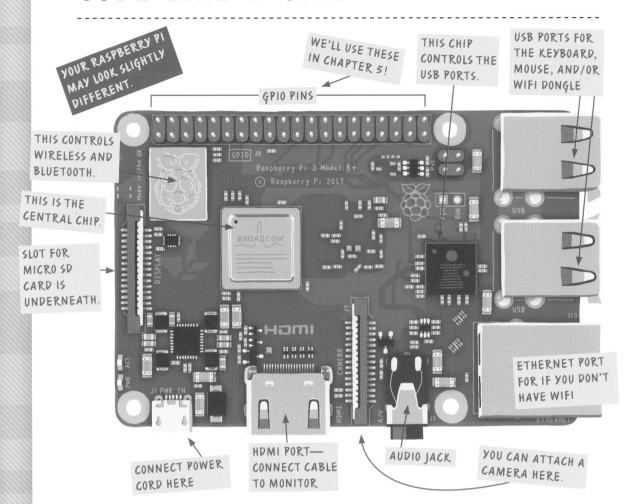

YOUR RASPBERRY PI MAY LOOK SLIGHTLY DIFFERENT.

WE'LL USE THESE IN CHAPTER 5!

THIS CHIP CONTROLS THE USB PORTS.

USB PORTS FOR THE KEYBOARD, MOUSE, AND/OR WIFI DONGLE

GPIO PINS

THIS CONTROLS WIRELESS AND BLUETOOTH.

THIS IS THE CENTRAL CHIP.

SLOT FOR MICRO SD CARD IS UNDERNEATH.

ETHERNET PORT FOR IF YOU DON'T HAVE WIFI

CONNECT POWER CORD HERE

HDMI PORT— CONNECT CABLE TO MONITOR

AUDIO JACK

YOU CAN ATTACH A CAMERA HERE.

CHALLENGE 2

Uh-Oh, the HDMI Cable Won't Plug into My Screen

HDMI stands for "high-definition multimedia interface." It's the same cable that most TVs use to send images and graphics to a screen. One end connects to the Raspberry Pi computer. If you're hooking up to a TV screen with an HDMI port—like what gaming systems connect to—chances are a simple "HDMI-to-HDMI" cable will work right away. Problem solved.

Sometimes, though, when you're using older screens and monitors, the HDMI cable doesn't fit. That's frustrating. You want to get your new computer up and running, but you've hit a roadblock. The things that look most ordinary can also be what make us want to tear our hair out.

So much of the Internet feels wireless and invisible, but actually, there's lots of physical gear that makes communication between screens, computers and keyboards possible.

What to do? First of all, keep calm and get ready to troubleshoot! The solution: find an HDMI cable with the right kind of plug on the other end, or add an adapter that makes the connections work.

HDMI-TO-HDMI CABLE. BOTH ENDS ARE THE SAME.

This may seem like a diversion, but I promise: once you're able to figure out cables, plugs and adapters, you'll have one of those awesome life skills no one tells you about. You have no idea how many problems are solved by understanding cables because: communication. Computing devices communicate, just like we humans do! Odd-looking cables will never bother you again. You will be able to Make. Things. Work.

If you go to a store or search online for "HDMI cables and adapters," you will probably find hundreds.

Who knew a cable could be such a mystery, right? Here's what to do: Sketch or snap a photo of the screen's receptacle, or *port,* for the HDMI plug. Notice whether the port has holes or pins, and what kind of shape surrounds the pins. Count the number of pins and how many rows of pins there are.

You can do this! Your reward is getting your own computer.

Now you can find your cable's name by searching for a match online or by going to a store that sells electronics. Two usual options are VGA and DVI, but, unfortunately, both come in several shapes and versions. One will match what you need: it may be a special kind of HDMI cable with the right end built in, or it may be a cable plus an adapter.

What now? I'm not making this up: it's time to figure out whether your cable is a boy or a girl.

You Won't Believe This

Plugs come in male and female versions. Yes, people have given plugs and ports a gender! Your cable or adapter will be named something like "male DVI to HDMI" or "HDMI to female VGA" or "male DVI-D to male HDMI."

Do the pins stick out? Yes? Well, that's a male plug. Does the plug have openings? Yes? That's a female plug! I know. Really. I will bet almost anything that women and girls were not at the table coming up with these names.

SO-CALLED "MALE" DVI CABLE

SO-CALLED "FEMALE" DVI CABLE

I Am Not a Genius Superstar

Tech is about things that don't work the first time. Tech and the Internet and machines have to communicate, and that communication doesn't always work. If setting up your Raspberry Pi computer works on the first try, know that a miracle has occurred.

I'd love to tell you that I'm a genius superstar at all this, but I've been learning as I go, just like you. My first time setting up a Raspberry Pi computer? Everything went wrong. I didn't understand the thing I just told you, about the HDMI cable. I ordered the wrong adapter—it was male when it needed to be female. I stopped by an electronics store, where the saleswoman sold me a much more expensive "converter," which I later realized I didn't need and which didn't work anyway. I returned it. When I eventually found the correct adapter, it cost less than $10, and then everything worked.

Much of a tech journey is spent in trial and error. You troubleshoot the problems. You search for the right plug and the correct lines of code. This is normal. Why keep at it? Because when you figure it out, you're the hero who saves the day. That feels fantastic.

My Raspberry Pi goof-ups continued. I jammed in the micro SD card, and it broke. My bad. I ordered a new card. That card didn't have the right software installed. I spent the next 5 hours searching the Raspberry Pi website and learning how to download the Raspbian operating system myself. Another time, I finally got everything connected, using my TV screen. I reveled in playing Minecraft, Raspberry Pi—edition, and building games on Scratch. Then the TV stopped working, which turned out to be a coincidence that was unrelated to the Raspberry Pi computer, but still.

In most of these cases, I was sure the computer was defective.

I was wrong.

I know I was wrong because one day the stars aligned. I followed directions and connected the cords in the right sequence. The screen on the new monitor lit up, the operating system loaded, and I tell you, it was magic.

I felt like I could do anything.

FRUSTRATION

Maybe setting up a Raspberry Pi computer will be easier for you than it was for me, but if you're experiencing some frustration, know that it is totally normal, and even expected. What to do?

1. Put on some music and dance.

2. Breathe. In through your nose, deep into your belly and out through your mouth, 3 times.

3. Jump up and down.

4. "Go wide." Think about other things, and get some perspective. This can work wonders.

5. Read the directions again, very slowly and out loud.

6. Vent to a friend.

7. Ask a friend for advice.

8. Laugh with a friend. Laughing brings in more oxygen and relaxes you. Plus, with more oxygen, our brains can think better.

9. Be kind to yourself. Back away and return later. Success will happen, just not right now.

10. Talk out loud to yourself. Developers have taught me this trick, called "rubber duck" programming. Hearing your own voice helps you see things you missed before.

11. Dance again. Because dance-party problem-solving is the way to go.

12. Celebrate the small victories along the way.

CHALLENGE 3

Put It All Together

We're ready to launch. In front of you are cables and a keyboard, mouse and screen. The paper instructions are laid out, or you've searched for the Quick Start Guide on raspberrypi.org. Here's an overview of how to put it all together. It should make following the official directions much easier. You can also look back at the illustrations on pages 68 and 70.

1 If your Raspberry Pi computer came with square "heat sinks," attach them to the chips. Silicon chips work hard and get hot. That's why laptops and desktops have fans to cool things down. (Newer models have other ways to deal with heat.)

2 Connect the keyboard and the mouse to your Raspberry Pi computer's USB ports.

3 Insert the micro SD card into the slot underneath your Raspberry Pi computer. If you have an older model, connect a WiFi dongle to the USB port or an Ethernet cord to the Ethernet port.

4 Plug the HDMI cable into the monitor or TV screen. Then plug the HDMI cable into the HDMI port of your Raspberry Pi computer.

5 TIP: You probably already know this, but if you're working with a TV, make sure to tune your TV to the stream that matches the port you're plugged into, like HDMI1 or HDMI2.

6 Power up! First plug the power cord into the Raspberry Pi computer, and then plug it into the wall.

When the power flows, the LED on the Raspberry Pi computer should turn on, and the screen should come alive. You may see tips, like username = pi and password = raspberry or the raspberry icon, and possibly even screen after screen of green writing on a black background. Once the operating system loads, the Raspberry Pi desktop will appear on your screen.

When that happens, you're good to go. You just put together your own computer.

WAIT, MINE ISN'T WORKING YET

The screen may go black or rainbow for a while. That's okay. If the scrolling stops and you get a "this isn't working" feeling in the pit of your stomach, type **startx** and see if that helps.

THE BIG PICTURE

In a nutshell, computers are about input, storage and processing, and output. That's exactly what the Raspberry Pi computer does. Imagine it as a creature that can take things in, store them, do things to them and send them back into the world in a different form. We push in data and commands, using a keyboard and mouse (or, as we'll see in Chapter 5, using sensors). The screen allows us to see what the computer is doing.

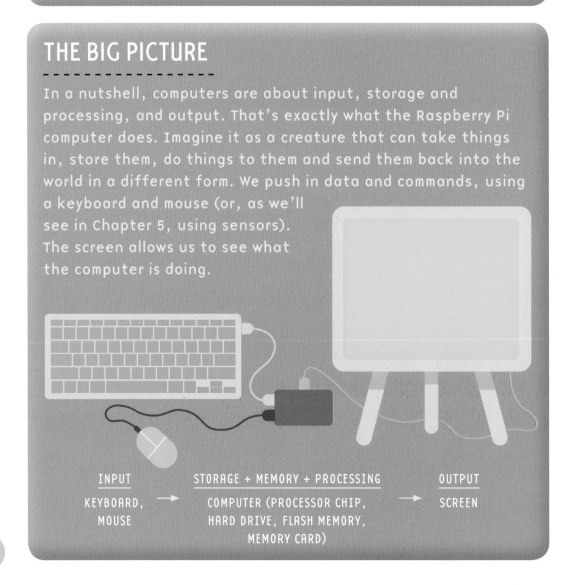

INPUT		STORAGE + MEMORY + PROCESSING		OUTPUT
KEYBOARD, MOUSE	→	COMPUTER (PROCESSOR CHIP, HARD DRIVE, FLASH MEMORY, MEMORY CARD)	→	SCREEN

CLICK
HERE
FOR
THE
MENU
BELOW.

FILE MANAGER

INTERNET

TERMINAL

What Now?

The Raspberry Pi desktop is preloaded with a universe of apps and goodies, things like Minecraft, Scratch, places to write and draw and code, a music app called Sonic Pi and more.

Connect to the Internet

Look for the connection to Wifi on the lower right-hand corner of your screen. Once you're connected, click the Globe button to get to the Raspberry Pi's Internet browser, which is Chromium.

Explore! Try every button. For tutorials, head over to raspberrypi.org/resources. Or click Help on the main menu.

IN TECH, THINGS CHANGE ALL THE TIME. YOUR MENU MAY LOOK A LITTLE DIFFERENT.

Q A video is streaming, but there's no sound. What's wrong?

A Have you plugged speakers or headphones into the audio jack? Still not working? Check the settings at Menu > Preferences > Audio Device Settings.

Minecraft

More and more girls are getting into Minecraft, and your Raspberry Pi computer comes with a free version, where you can build villages, landscapes, theme parks and nearly anything you can imagine.

Spawn into a rock-cliff biome and dig out a many-leveled cave home. Find it at Games › Minecraft.

Scratch

Go to Programming › Scratch. It may look different from the Web version we learned in Chapter 1, but you can still do your Scratch projects here.

Write and Draw

From the Raspberry Pi menu, click on Office. There you'll find the LibreOffice apps for writing, drawing, making slide shows and much more. Welcome to a free, parallel universe to Microsoft Office! It's brought to you by developers around the globe who believe in free and open-source software.

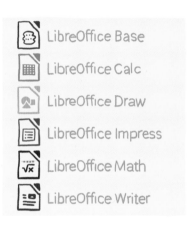

LibreOffice Base
LibreOffice Calc
LibreOffice Draw
LibreOffice Impress
LibreOffice Math
LibreOffice Writer

Sonic Pi

At Programming › Sonic Pi, you can use the coding language Ruby to compose music. To get started: google "getting started with Sonic Pi," check out sonic-pi.net, and watch this YouTube video: Geek Gurl Diaries, "How to Code Music with Raspberry Pi & Sonic Pi."

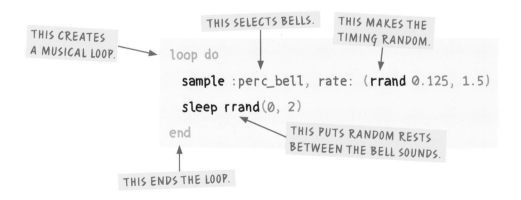

THIS CREATES A MUSICAL LOOP.

THIS SELECTS BELLS.

THIS MAKES THE TIMING RANDOM.

```
loop do
    sample :perc_bell, rate: (rrand 0.125, 1.5)
    sleep rrand(0, 2)
end
```

THIS PUTS RANDOM RESTS BETWEEN THE BELL SOUNDS.

THIS ENDS THE LOOP.

UH-OH, SOME OF MY KEYBOARD KEYS DON'T WORK

Press the **#** key. If it (or others) doesn't work, it's not that your keyboard is broken; it's that your Raspberry Pi computer is British! Time to explore the settings. Go to **Menu > Preferences > Raspberry Pi Configuration > Localisation > Set Keyboard**. Reset the keyboard to U.S., or to wherever you are in the world. Check out the other controls, too. Click on country names and see your keyboard language change to Thai, Nepalese, Arabic, Urdu and other alphabets.

Last but Not Least, Terminal

The same night I first learned about Raspberry Pi, my friend Meredith showed me something else: Terminal.

Terminal is a super-powerful behind-the-scenes place on your computer that most people don't even know about. Developers use it all the time to install software, run programs and create new files and folders. Typing commands into Terminal definitely makes you feel like a pro.

See $, the dollar sign? It's the prompt, and we can type commands in after it. (That's why this line is called the command line.)

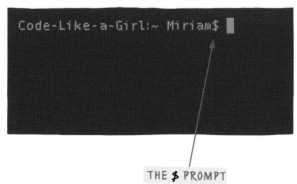

THIS IS WHAT TERMINAL LOOKS LIKE.

Code-Like-a-Girl:~ Miriam$

THE $ PROMPT

Let's use Terminal to update the software that the Raspberry Pi computer runs on.

1 To open Terminal, click this button or, on the menu, go to Accessories › Terminal.

2 At the $ prompt, type the first line given below. Press Enter. Wait for the $ prompt to reappear, type the next line, press Enter, and then type the final line to reboot. . . .

```
sudo apt-get update
sudo apt-get dist-upgrade
sudo reboot
```

Terminal may ask you for the Pi password, which is "raspberry."

Q What's *sudo*?

A **Super**user **do**. It means the person in charge of the computer: you.

What's going on? With these commands in Terminal, we are communicating with the Internet and getting the newest version of the Raspbian operating system and desktop. Then we use a command to tell the system to reboot—or turn off and on again. Pretty amazing!

Intrigued? Google "Terminal and Raspberry Pi" for more tips and tricks, including some awesome Easter eggs hidden there.

Dear Reader,

Why does this matter? Once I was at a White House conference (really!), listening to a talk by Megan Smith. She's a former Google executive who, in 2014, became the first female chief technology officer of the United States. She was excited to tell us about the women who created some of the hardware and software that we use today. She began with Ada Lovelace (1815–1852), the world's first computer programmer.

Q Whoa. Ada Lovelace died in 1852, way before computers were invented.

A Ada worked closely with Charles Babbage on his Analytical Engine. He never got to build it, but she provided the insights that became the basis for computer programming.

During World War II, a team of U.S. women in their twenties created the first software. A team of men had built computing machines and afterward had no idea how to use them. These women were actually called "computers," because they had been hired to do mathematical computation. Across the Atlantic, in Britain's Bletchley Park, women like Joan Clarke, Margaret Rock, Mavis Lever and Ruth Briggs worked long hours with Alan Turing to program his new computer to break codes and locate German submarines. All of these women helped turn World War II around into a victory for the Allies.

Check out the video memories of women who worked in Britain by googling "women code breakers of Bletchley Park."

CODE LIKE A GIRL

At the same time, in Boston, a navy officer named Grace Hopper was writing software with a team at Harvard University. She went on to lead the team that created the programming language COBOL.

> Know who said "If it's a good idea, go ahead and do it. It's much easier to apologize than it is to get permission"? Grace Hopper!

Megan Smith also told us about Joanna Hoffman and Susan Kare, who were on the team that developed the original Apple computer, and Katherine Johnson, born in 1918, who worked on Apollo 11 with her mathematician colleagues and friends. When the movie *Hidden Figures* came out in 2016, it turned Katherine Johnson into a celebrity and made her friends Dorothy Vaughan and Mary Jackson, and the other women they worked with, into beloved and inspiring heroes.

With code and tech, you can build amazing things for the world. That's why next up is full-on coding with the Python® programming language.

 LOVE, MIRIAM

FEARLESS SEARCHING

Part of the tech journey is feeling ready to try stuff. Banish all fear! Nothing you do can break the Internet. It's even hard to break a device unless you smash it or douse it with water. Stuck on something? Look it up online. Many people will have asked similar questions before and will have answers for you. Search for everything you need!

CHAPTER 3

CODING WITH PYTHON®

Dear Reader,

"**C**omputers are stupid."

That's what I heard the other night, when I took a Python programming language workshop from a guy named Brad. You see, I went on a journey to learn all of this, in order to bring it to you. I mean, if a non-techy, non-mathy person like me can learn to code, then all of us can. Brad sported a Death Star T-shirt and dark glasses, but he was a really nice guy. We met upstairs at a hipster makerspace with silver bathrooms. "None of this is intuitive," Brad said as he began to teach us about webscraping. "You have to figure out each

piece. Read the manual. Then it builds. And you know what?
Senior developers google stuff all the time. Even more than junior
developers."

> Webscraping is one way that code can grab information and
> data from websites, like movie times or sports scores or
> daily meditations or the latest stories from teenvogue.com.
> You and I can't webscrape yet—it's beyond the basics, but
> totally awesome.

He reassured us that anyone can code. "It's not meant to be tricky," he
said. "Computers are stupid and nothing to be afraid of."

Well, then.

We're about to high-dive into Python, an honest-to-goodness grown-up
programming language that runs nearly a third of the Internet. Sites like
Pinterest, Instagram, Dropbox, Google and YouTube have been built on
Python. At newspapers, journalists use Python to track down statistics and
numbers so they can report powerful stories.

I promised to send up a warning flare when things got harder, so here
it is. Python is a language that real developers use, and there is definitely
a transition from Scratch to this kind of code. If it feels hard at first, that's
okay. It *is* hard. Hard is good. Hard is awesome! You feel like a hero
when you're done. I've tried to forge an upbeat path into Python for us,
but if it's tough to wrap your mind around all of it, don't think you've
become dumb overnight and that you're stressing over something simple.
Promise me you'll keep going.

I'll show you one example of what we're in for. In Scratch, to run a program that makes an elephant jump up and down 10 times, you'd drag over a loop that looks like this:

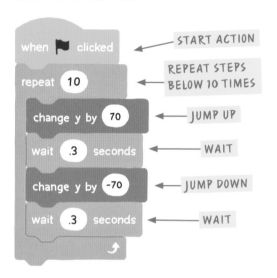

START ACTION

REPEAT STEPS BELOW 10 TIMES

JUMP UP

WAIT

JUMP DOWN

WAIT

Right? Start the action. Call in a repeat loop. Change the elephant's position so she jumps up. Wait, then change her position so she jumps down. Wait . . . and the loop starts over.

Get ready! Here goes Python's version of a repeat loop:

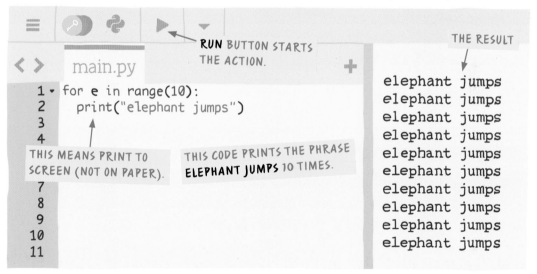

RUN BUTTON STARTS THE ACTION.

THE RESULT

main.py

```
1  for e in range(10):
2     print("elephant jumps")
3
4
```

THIS MEANS PRINT TO SCREEN (NOT ON PAPER).

THIS CODE PRINTS THE PHRASE ELEPHANT JUMPS 10 TIMES.

```
elephant jumps
elephant jumps
elephant jumps
elephant jumps
elephant jumps
elephant jumps
elephant jumps
elephant jumps
elephant jumps
elephant jumps
```

I know. Totally different. Instead of a colorful loop, there's an odd phrase—for e in range(10):—and in Python, it's called a for loop. A second line adds the function print, as in: print the phrase "elephant jumps." The formula looks weird, and there's no actual picture of an elephant; we have to imagine it.

CODE LIKE A GIRL

With Scratch, we did the behind-the-scenes programming *and* we saw the front-end result. It looked great on-screen. With Python, we're behind the scenes the whole time, because Python is a back-end language. We see the results in the Terminal, also called a console or shell.

Don't worry about understanding everything the first few times through. If this feels new and unfamiliar, you're in great company. We'll get there together. I'll show you *where* we write and run Python code, and we'll code some programs, and maybe by the end, you'll be changing the code on your own. That's when those "aha" moments hit.

Brad's comment that computers are stupid? What he meant was they're extremely literal, and in any programming language, we have to write code in a specific order and with an exact combo of letters, numbers and characters.

That's what we're about to do.

 LOVE, MIRIAM

P.S. That manual Brad mentioned? It's at python.org. Click on Documentation (and when you finish this chapter, look at their Beginner's Guide).

Python Turtles

Some people might start with a boring Python project, but not us. Let's cast on with a touch of color and playfulness. See these?

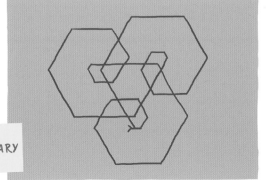

PYTHON HAS A SPECIAL "TURTLE-GRAPHICS" LIBRARY THAT MAKES THESE!

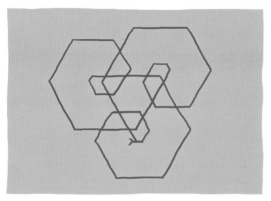 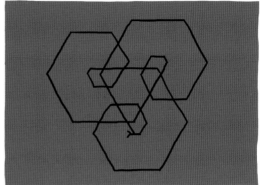

We're going to make them with Python.

First, though, we've got to answer the getting-started-in-tech mystery: Where do you write and run code? In videos, hackers type away in black computer windows with colorful lines of code. But where do you find that magical space?

Uh-Oh! There's a Big Mystery!

With Scratch, everything you need to write and run code is at scratch.mit.edu. For Python and other languages, it's not so simple. You can *write* code anywhere: a napkin, a sidewalk, a window! Professional programmers use a text editor and their computer's Terminal, and other things, called IDEs, that are a bit more complicated than beginners usually want. What *do* we want? To code in a spot that's easy to use and that we can get to from any device, including our smartphones. That's right. If the mood strikes, we want to be able to code on a smartphone.

I started my search for a cozy place where we can write and run Python that's easy to use and accessible to all.

When I told my new developer-friends what I was looking for, they shook their heads. "You should only code Python on an actual computer," they said.

I believed them and kept searching anyway. This, I realized, is exactly what coding is about: having an idea and going for it, no matter what. Sure enough, I lit upon trinket.io. I think you'll love coding here.

> This is what coding is all about—not taking no for an answer, and finding your way in.

Trinket was created by a programmer who studied art history in college and learned to code at age 27. The site is lovely, user-friendly and free (for us). Best of all, Elliott Hauser and the team programmed it with a special trick: any device you have, type trinket.io into a browser and you can use it to program Python (and other languages, too).

Problem solved.

SIGN UP, LOG IN, THEN CLICK ON YOUR ACCOUNT NAME TO FIND A PLACE TO CODE.

Share Code from any Device

Trinket lets you run and write code in any browser, on any device.
Trinkets work instantly, with no need to log in, download plugins, or install software.
Easily share or embed the code with your changes when you're done.

Turtles, Take Two

Let's go! Open a browser, type trinket.io and create an account. (You'll need an email address, so if you don't have one, ask a parent or guardian about setting one up.) Once you're in Trinket, poke around, figure out where things are and explore the tutorials.

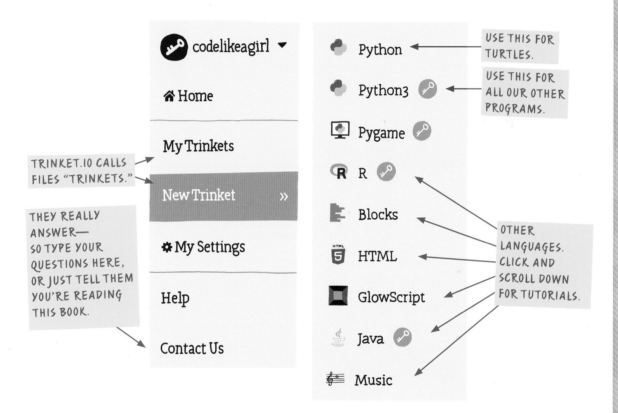

Now for the turtles. Turtles have a vaunted place in the history of programming. In Logo, one of the first educational coding languages, kids would learn to code by moving turtles around the screen. Google "turtles and Python" or "turtle art" and you'll see.

Why turtles? Because of the Mock Turtle in *Alice's Adventures in Wonderland*—a book the creator of Logo loved.

CODE LIKE A GIRL

To get started, click New Trinket and then click Python, then click or tap (if you're on a phone or tablet!) into the main editing window. This is where we'll write the code that's on page 91. When you're done, save your code, and click (or tap) the Run button.

> Confusion Alert! Use the Python button for this project . . . but for all the next projects, we'll click the **Python 3** button to get started.

Q Hold on. There's more than one Python? What's up with that?

A Here's the story: Python was released in 1991. Things were going along pretty much fine, with updates and new versions, like Python 2, when in late 2008, Python's developer—his name is Guido van Rossum—pushed out the next version, Python 3. It was a big deal.

Did all the Python programmers say, "Hey, Guido! Thanks, dude. We'll make the switch"? Of course not! Many continued to code with Python 2. This is normal. The Internet is brimming with both cutting-edge new code and old code that programmers patch together to make it work.

Q How do we know which one to use?

A Once again I surveyed my Python programmer pals. "We mostly use Python 2 right now," my new tech friends told me. "Eventually everyone will switch over. Go with the future." I chose Python 3. (Except for turtles, that is, which works better on Python 2.)

RUN BUTTON

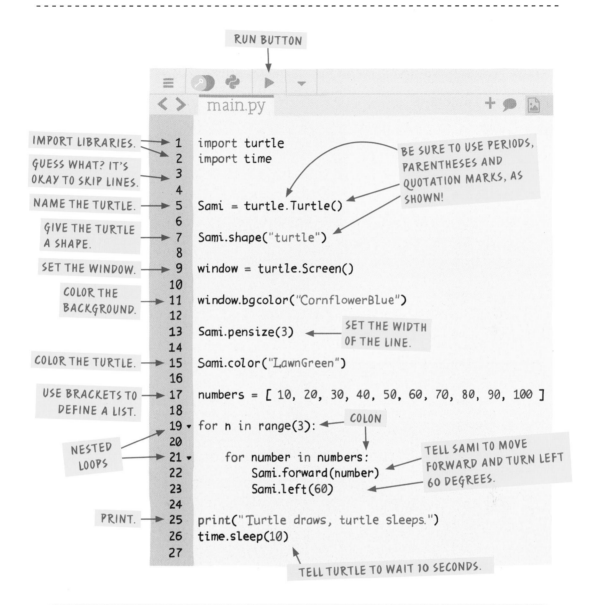

main.py

IMPORT LIBRARIES.
```
1  import turtle
2  import time
```

GUESS WHAT? IT'S OKAY TO SKIP LINES.
```
3
4
```

BE SURE TO USE PERIODS, PARENTHESES AND QUOTATION MARKS, AS SHOWN!

NAME THE TURTLE.
```
5  Sami = turtle.Turtle()
6
```

GIVE THE TURTLE A SHAPE.
```
7  Sami.shape("turtle")
8
```

SET THE WINDOW.
```
9  window = turtle.Screen()
10
```

COLOR THE BACKGROUND.
```
11 window.bgcolor("CornflowerBlue")
12
```

SET THE WIDTH OF THE LINE.
```
13 Sami.pensize(3)
14
```

COLOR THE TURTLE.
```
15 Sami.color("LawnGreen")
16
```

USE BRACKETS TO DEFINE A LIST.
```
17 numbers = [ 10, 20, 30, 40, 50, 60, 70, 80, 90, 100 ]
18
```

COLON
```
19 for n in range(3):
20
```

NESTED LOOPS
```
21     for number in numbers:
22         Sami.forward(number)
23         Sami.left(60)
24
```

TELL SAMI TO MOVE FORWARD AND TURN LEFT 60 DEGREES.

PRINT.
```
25 print("Turtle draws, turtle sleeps.")
26 time.sleep(10)
27
```

TELL TURTLE TO WAIT 10 SECONDS.

My turtle is named Sami. Feel free to choose your turtle's name—and be sure to insert the new name on lines 5, 7, 13, 15, 22 and 23.

CODE LIKE A GIRL

Click the triangular Run button, and your turtle should start drawing this shape!

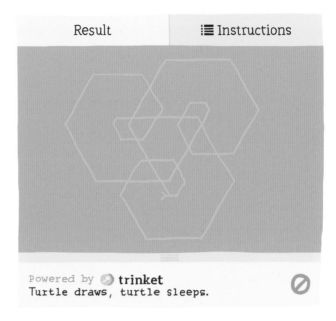

Result   ≣ Instructions

Powered by 🌀 **trinket**
Turtle draws, turtle sleeps.

CHANGE COLORS

Lines 11 and 15 set color for the background and for the turtle. Browsers can understand some color names, like:

- AliceBlue
- Aqua
- BlueViolet
- Chocolate
- DarkGray
- DeepSkyBlue
- ForestGreen

- GhostWhite
- Goldenrod
- GreenYellow
- LightGreen
- LightSteelBlue
- Orange
- Orchid

- PeachPuff
- Plum
- RosyBrown
- SandyBrown
- SlateBlue
- Tomato
- Wheat

To make all the color shades, digital designers also use Hex codes and RGB values. The Hex system uses combinations of letters and numbers. RGB stands for the primary colors Red-Green-Blue. In these systems, the name SlateBlue is the same as the Hex code #6A5ACD, which is also the same as RGB(106, 90, 205). For more, google "Web colors."

MORE CHANGES TO TRY!

★ See line 7 on page 91, which reads `Sami.shape("turtle")`? You can change "turtle" to "arrow", "circle", "square" or "classic".

★ Line 17 controls the length of each section of the shape. Try out some other numbers and see what happens.

★ Line 23 controls the angle and direction of change. Try swapping 60 degrees for 20, 36, 45, 90 or any number up to 360.

★ Where you see words like forward and left, substitute backward and right.

OMG, Announcing a New, Official "Hello World!"

Let's make this coding thing our own. Click into Python 3, which is what we'll use from here on in. This time around, let's improve on "Hello World!" There's a new first-code phrase in town: "Look out world, here we come!"

Type this line of code and click the arrow to run. We are on our way.

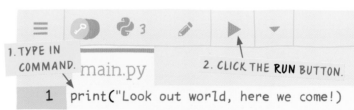

1. TYPE IN COMMAND. main.py

2. CLICK THE RUN BUTTON.

```
1    print("Look out world, here we come!)
```

Wait, what just happened? An error?! That can't be. The computer must be wrong. . . .

ERROR MESSAGE TELLS US TO LOOK AT LINE 1.

≣ Instructions

Powered by 🔵 trinket   ⊘
```
    File
"/tmp/sessions/f9f222924ebc1b02/main.py",
line 1
      print("Look out world, here we come!)
                                           ^
SyntaxError: EOL while scanning string
literal
```

HERE'S THE CLUE. THE CARET POINTS TO THE PROBLEM.

THAT'S IT! THE CLOSING QUOTATION MARK IS MISSING.

SYNTAX MEANS THE GRAMMAR AND RULES OF A PROGRAMMING LANGUAGE.

EOL MEANS END OF LINE.

STRING = WHAT'S INSIDE THE QUOTATION MARKS.

CODE LIKE A GIRL

Okay, I admit, I did this on purpose to show what happens when code doesn't work. The result? Nothing terrible. Deafening alarms don't ring. Smoke doesn't pour from the sides of your device. It's just a line of code that can't run. As we say in my house, "No problem. Just fix it."

ERRORS = NO BIG DEAL

To code means to solve one problem after another. In the code on page 93, Python sends us a message about the error. It looks weird, but it's really saying: "Hey, here's the name of the file, and here's the line that's not working. By the way, we found the error at the EOL, which means end of line. You might also want to know we caught this while scanning the string literal or, more simply, the words you typed in."

I'll explain strings in a moment, but basically, it's the name—or data type—for words and characters.

In short, I left out the second quotation mark in "Look out world, here we come!" Many code errors are just like this. One tiny quotation mark or semicolon goes missing. There are 2 dots or backslashes when there should only be 1. Remember "computers are stupid"? In code, every character must be in the absolute right place. When it's not, your program will not make pouty faces. Or get judgy. Or talk about you behind your back. It'll just return an error message that, with any luck, gives you a useful hint about what went wrong. What to do? Find and fix the error. Run the program again.

That's right. Make an error, fix an error. No big deal.

So let's fix the code by adding the missing quotation mark, and we're good to go. Press the Run button again.

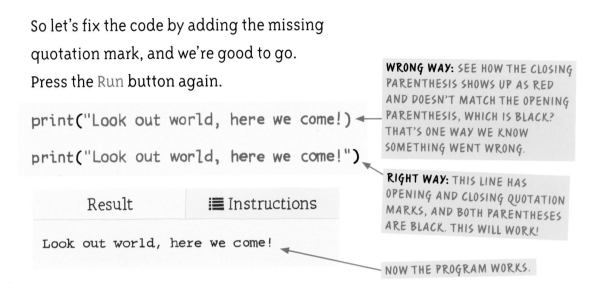

```
print("Look out world, here we come!)
print("Look out world, here we come!")
```

WRONG WAY: SEE HOW THE CLOSING PARENTHESIS SHOWS UP AS RED AND DOESN'T MATCH THE OPENING PARENTHESIS, WHICH IS BLACK? THAT'S ONE WAY WE KNOW SOMETHING WENT WRONG.

RIGHT WAY: THIS LINE HAS OPENING AND CLOSING QUOTATION MARKS, AND BOTH PARENTHESES ARE BLACK. THIS WILL WORK!

Result	☰ Instructions

```
Look out world, here we come!
```

NOW THE PROGRAM WORKS.

AgeFinder2050

Welcome to our AgeFinder app. Ever wonder how old you'll be in 2050? AgeFinder2050 asks for your birth year, does the math and reports back how old you'll be at midcentury.

Open a new Python 3 file, and code these lines. See if you can get the app to work—press Run and enter your birth year—and then I'll show you how it happens.

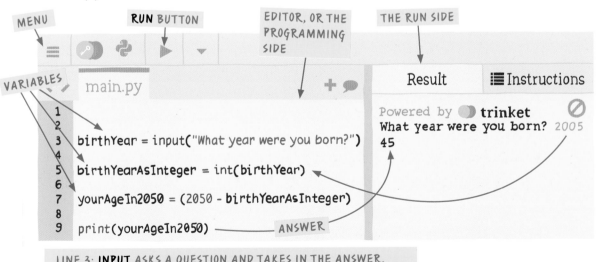

```
birthYear = input("What year were you born?")
birthYearAsInteger = int(birthYear)
yourAgeIn2050 = (2050 - birthYearAsInteger)
print(yourAgeIn2050)
```

LINE 3: **INPUT** ASKS A QUESTION AND TAKES IN THE ANSWER.
LINE 5: **INT** CHANGES THE YEAR YOU ENTERED INTO AN INTEGER.
LINE 7: SUBTRACT! HERE'S THE EQUATION WE NEED!

CODE LIKE A GIRL

Remember variables? The storage spots where you can put a piece of data? The words along the left—**birthYear**, **birthYearAsInteger** and **yourAgeIn2050**—are variables. They hold the original piece of information—your birth year—as the program processes it.

1 You enter your birth year, 2005. It's stored in the variable called birthYear. Get ready: this is a crazy tech thing. It looks like a whole number, or integer, to us. But Python doesn't yet see it that way. That means Python won't do math with our number until we officially change it into a data type called an integer.

2 That's why on line 5, birthYear gets tumbled around with a function called int(). That makes it an actual Python-approved integer data type. We store this in the second variable, called birthYearAsInteger.

3 Finally, birthYearAsInteger gets tumbled around with some subtraction. Python takes this new result and stores it in memory as the third variable: yourAgeIn2050.

Q Why are there 3 variables?

A Imagine a factory. One person brings cloth to a machine. The machine cuts it. Then the cut cloth is carried to another machine. This second machine sews up the sides. The sewn cloth is brought to a third machine, which attaches buttons. In other words, a new variable/storage spot holds each stage of the process.

Q But where's the answer?

A The final answer is stored inside the yourAgeIn2050 variable.

4 At the moment, we can't see the answer. That's because the variable yourAgeIn2050 is storing it in memory. When we finally use the print function that's on line 9—look back at the code on page 95—we'll see on screen that if you were born in 2005, you'll be 45 in 2050.

THE RESULT!

QUESTION FROM LINE 1 → `What year were you born?` 2005 ← YOU ENTER YOUR BIRTH YEAR.

`45`

↑ THE ANSWER!

This process is the power of programming, and you'll see it over and over. Your code takes in data, does things to it and returns the result. You could have done this math yourself, but now you've built a tool that can do this party trick forever, with anyone's birth year.

DATA TYPES

You've got your pants, your tops, your skirts. You've got a jacket and a sweater. These are your clothes types. You don't use your jeans as a winter coat, and you don't use socks as your belt. Same with data types. A program wants to know which type of data it's using. Some common Python data types are:

1 Integers, or whole numbers, such as 1, 3, 36, 795.

2 Floats, which are numbers with decimals, such as 3.45 or 1032.453.

3 Strings, which are letters, words, characters and spaces.
★★Strings always have quotation marks around them.★★

TYPING

Coding definitely goes faster when you know how to touch-type.
To learn, try:

* Dance Mat Typing—to find it, google "Dance Mat Typing."
* Typing.io, which is typing practice with actual code!
* On a tablet, search "best apps for learning to type on an iPad/
  Android," whichever you have.

TIPS AND TRICKS

* Each key is assigned to a specific finger.

* You don't have to type fast. Typing slowly and getting it right is
  better than speed-typing and then spending 20 minutes looking
  for a hard-to-find mistake.

* Use your voice. Say the key-finger connection out loud: "K is
  the right-hand second finger." "Q is the left-hand pinky."

"Plus sign is left pinky on Shift and right pinky on the plus key."
"Period is the right-hand third finger" and so on.

* What about the numbers and symbols along the top? Stretch your fingers to reach up. To type the symbols above the numbers, hold the Shift key with one pinky and use the other hand's fingers to type.

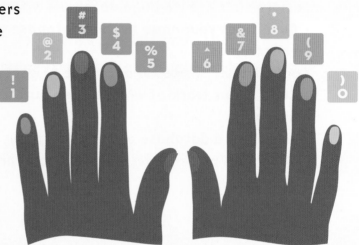

I'M USED TO A TABLET
If you've mostly been using a phone or a tablet, typing at the computer will involve a few new skills.

1 Practice touch-typing, of course.

2 Take some time to figure out how the mouse or touchpad works.

3 Learn to use the Command and Control buttons to copy and paste text. (Whether it's Command or Control depends on your machine, so you'll have to experiment.)

To select a chunk of text, click at the beginning and drag to the end of the section. To select all text on a page, hold down Command (or Control) + A.

To copy: Command (or Control) + C.

To paste into a new place, move the cursor there and hold down: Command (or Control) + V.

Doesn't work? Google "copy and paste" and "keyboard tricks" for the computer you're using.

Change, or Going for 2.0

Life changes all the time. That's true for code, too. Often, as soon as we get code working, we think up a new feature to add. After I finished this app and tried it a few times, and then sent it to a friend to get her feedback, I thought about how to improve it.

Usually with dice, you don't just roll once, but many times. I decided to add a playAgain feature. If a person answers yes, or y, the program runs again. If she answers no, or n, the user gets a message to have a great day. Since this is a situation with "ifs," I used an if-else statement—aka a conditional—to show the program how to take in the yes-or-no answer and use it to make the right decision.

Change your code, too, and give this new version a spin.

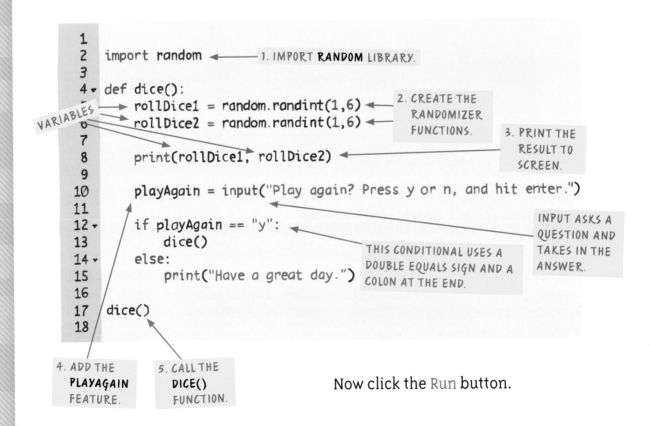

```
1
2    import random          ←  1. IMPORT RANDOM LIBRARY.
3
4 ▾  def dice():
5        rollDice1 = random.randint(1,6)    ←  2. CREATE THE
6        rollDice2 = random.randint(1,6)    ←     RANDOMIZER
7                                                  FUNCTIONS.
8        print(rollDice1, rollDice2)   ←  3. PRINT THE
9                                          RESULT TO
10       playAgain = input("Play again? Press y or n, and hit enter.")    SCREEN.
11
12 ▾     if playAgain == "y":
13           dice()
14 ▾     else:
15           print("Have a great day.")
16
17 /  dice()
18
```

VARIABLES

THIS CONDITIONAL USES A DOUBLE EQUALS SIGN AND A COLON AT THE END.

INPUT ASKS A QUESTION AND TAKES IN THE ANSWER.

4. ADD THE **PLAYAGAIN** FEATURE.

5. CALL THE **DICE()** FUNCTION.

Now click the Run button.

```
4 4
Play again? Press y or n, and
hit enter. y
6 6
Play again? Press y or n, and
hit enter. y
2 1
Play again? Press y or n, and
hit enter. y
4 3
Play again? Press y or n, and
hit enter. n
Have a great day.
```

THE RESULTS

Lazy Developers

Developers like to say they are lazy. If given a chance, they'll write fewer lines of code, rather than more. That's why we defined a brand-new function and gave it the name dice(). This way, we can tell our app to roll the dice without rewriting all those lines. With our new dice() function, we just write dice() and we're done.

That's right. Lines 4–15 define our new dice() function. It puts a lot of actions and variables inside. Line 17 runs the dice() function, and it also runs on line 13.

That's why lazy developers write their own functions all the time. They also use libraries. These are collections of functions. See line 2, where it says import random? That imports a bunch of functions that pick random items and numbers.

Q What does import mean? Why doesn't Python just come with all the functions?

A Programs don't want to get bogged down with extra lines of code they don't always need. It makes them run more slowly, and that's not good. That's why we import special libraries of code.

YOU'RE CRUSHING IT!

You now know 4 of the 5 basic elements of programming!

1 Loops = repeats.

2 Variables = storage bins.

3 Conditionals = if-else statements.

4 Functions = actions. They're like verbs in sentences. They come ready-made, or you can create your own.

5 Lists, aka arrays (still to come).

Q Wait, I don't really understand libraries yet.

A It's like a book library, except that instead of borrowing books or movies, we borrow functions. Python and other languages come with many built-in functions. When we want more functions, such as a randomizer, or timers, or turtles, we import them through libraries.

Magic 8 Ball ®

I always have big questions about life, and small practical ones, too. If you do, too—and really, who doesn't?—let's build an app that's similar to a Magic 8 Ball toy to give us the answers we seek. For inspiration, let's think about what a Magic 8 Ball does. You hold the ball, think or say a question, shake the ball, and wait for the message to float through the inky blue liquid till you can read it through the tiny window.

Want to build a Magic 8 Ball with code? Open up trinket.io, start a new Python 3 file and type out the following lines. Oh, and when you get to line 13, I brainstormed these answers, but go on and make up your own. Just use the same format.

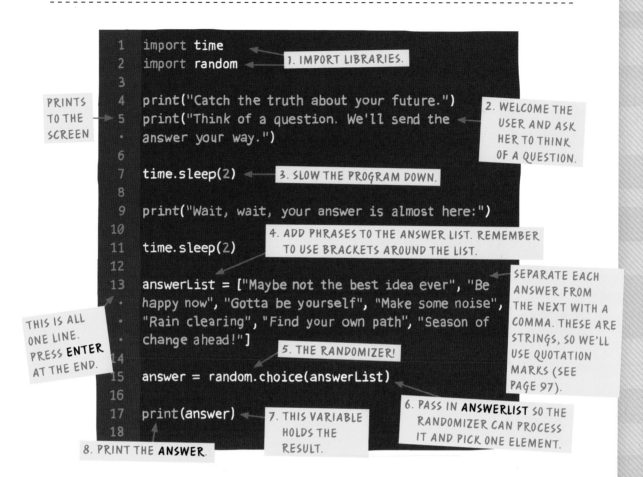

```
1    import time
2    import random                  1. IMPORT LIBRARIES.
3
4    print("Catch the truth about your future.")
5    print("Think of a question. We'll send the
     answer your way.")
6
7    time.sleep(2)                   3. SLOW THE PROGRAM DOWN.
8
9    print("Wait, wait, your answer is almost here:")
10
11   time.sleep(2)
12
13   answerList = ["Maybe not the best idea ever", "Be
     happy now", "Gotta be yourself", "Make some noise",
     "Rain clearing", "Find your own path", "Season of
     change ahead!"]
14
15   answer = random.choice(answerList)
16
17   print(answer)
18
```

PRINTS TO THE SCREEN

2. WELCOME THE USER AND ASK HER TO THINK OF A QUESTION.

4. ADD PHRASES TO THE ANSWER LIST. REMEMBER TO USE BRACKETS AROUND THE LIST.

SEPARATE EACH ANSWER FROM THE NEXT WITH A COMMA. THESE ARE STRINGS, SO WE'LL USE QUOTATION MARKS (SEE PAGE 97).

THIS IS ALL ONE LINE. PRESS **ENTER** AT THE END.

5. THE RANDOMIZER!

6. PASS IN **ANSWERLIST** SO THE RANDOMIZER CAN PROCESS IT AND PICK ONE ELEMENT.

7. THIS VARIABLE HOLDS THE RESULT.

8. PRINT THE **ANSWER**.

THE RESULT

```
Catch the truth about your future.
Think of a question. We'll send the answer your way.

Wait, wait, your answer is almost here:

Make some noise.
```

WELCOME TEXT

WAIT MESSAGE

A RANDOMLY CHOSEN ANSWER JUST FOR YOU

See, the user never really enters an actual question, she just thinks it. And gets an answer.

BUT, MIRIAM, HOW DO YOU KNOW WHAT THE CODE SHOULD BE???

I don't, at the beginning. I start by thinking about a Magic 8 Ball. You ask a question, shake the ball and wait for an answer. That's the feeling I want to create with code: question, wait, answer.

The Formula really helps here. I'll figure out the steps and match each step with code that will bring it to life.

After I sketch out The Formula, I'll move the code into a text editor, like trinket.io, or others that I use at home. I'll make sure to put all the steps in order.

The Formula

ACTIONS AND QUESTIONS	PYTHON CODE
Welcome the player and ask her to think of a question.	Use the **print** function and craft some welcoming sentences: print("Catch the truth about your future.") print("Think of a question. We'll send the answer your way.")
Python will pick an answer very quickly. The **time** library has a **sleep** function that will slow things down so the answer won't show right away.	Put **import time** on line 1. Once that's done, call the **sleep** function to insert a 2-second pause, like this: time.sleep(2) This is similar to the Scratch **wait** block. wait (2) seconds

Add a line that says the answer is coming soon.	print("Wait, wait, your answer is almost here:")
Make a list that holds all the possible answers.	A variable holds one thing. A list, also called an array, has the superpower of holding many things. answerList = ["Maybe not the best idea ever", "Be happy now", "Gotta be yourself", "Make some noise", "Rain clearing", "Find your own path", "Season of change ahead!"]
Set up the randomizer to pick one of the answers each time.	Put **import random** on line 2, just below **import time**, so the libraries are at the top of the code. ★ Use the **random.choice()** function to pick a random element from the list. ★ Tell the function about the list by "passing it in." That means: put **answerList** inside the parentheses, like this: **random.choice(answerList)**. ★ Put the answer into a new variable: **answer = random.choice(answerList)**
Show the result on-screen.	We've done this before: **print(answer)**

Q In the final line, print(answer), why don't we use quotation marks around the word answer?

A Because here answer is a variable—it holds the actual answer inside. In Python, only strings—or words—are wrapped in quotation marks. Not variables. It's confusing, like crazy spelling rules in English, but you get used to it.

So this is how a program grows, one line at a time. Once you get this version working, have fun with it. Want more? Search online for "Magic 8 Ball Answers" and code a 2.0 version with classic Magic 8 Ball answers, or your own answers. Don't worry about breaking your code. You can always return to the original and start over.

Reader: Will I ever get this?
Magic 8 Ball: "It is certain."
Serious answer: Yes. Just keep at it. With practice, code starts to feel more familiar.

Why Are These Programs and Apps So Ugly?

One question you may still be wondering about, though: Why are our apps so ugly? After all, web apps and mobile apps can be gorgeous. What are we missing?

It's ugly because we're writing back-end code and testing it in the Terminal, or console. Python is a "back-end" language—it calculates and processes the data we give it. In real life, the Magic 8 Ball app, or any of our Python programs, would be connected to a fully designed "front end." It would look like apps you use all the time.

I'll show you. Nearly every website makes you log in, right? That means a programmer has written back-end code that checks your password. Here's a super-simple example. Pretend we're on a team that's building an app called Dance Party. We want our users to enter a password, and we'll check to make sure it's long enough. (We could also match the email and password to our database, which would be encrypted and super secure, but that's beyond the basics!)

Here's some Python code for a pretend site called Dance Party. The code asks for your password and makes sure it's 8 characters or more. In trinket.io, create a new Python 3 file, and type in this code. It uses a function called len() to check the password's length. We'll also use some if-else logic to tell our program what to do.

```
1
2    password = input("Password, please?")    ← INPUT

4    if len(password) < 8:    ← MAKE SURE TO INCLUDE THE COLON.
5        print("Passwords must be 8 characters or more. Try again.")
6    else:
7        print("Welcome to the Dance Party!")
8
```

VARIABLE

CONDITIONAL

IF YOU ENTER A PASSWORD WITH TOO FEW CHARACTERS, THE PROGRAM TELLS YOU TO TRY AGAIN.

IF YOU ENTER A LONG ENOUGH PASSWORD, YOU GET A "WELCOME" MESSAGE.

```
Password, please?
    Wiggles
Passwords must be 8 characters or more. Try again.
```

TYPE IN A PASSWORD.

Wiggles, which is the name of my dog, is a very good dog but not a good password. This longer password should pass the length test:

```
Password, please?
    elephants@@    NEW PASSWORD
Welcome to the Dance Party!
```

CODE LIKE A GIRL

We've got the code working, and it's ugly like all the others! Now let's imagine the front end, which is the part people will see. Here's a design for the Dance Party web and mobile apps.

Dance Party!

Password: `Wiggles`

Passwords must be 8 characters or more. Try again.

Dance Party!

Password: `elephants@@`

Welcome to the Dance Party!

See? You'd enter the password, and our Python program would check that it's long enough. As a result, either you'd get in or be asked to try again.

> To learn more about front-end code, try khanacademy.org's Intro to HTML/CSS: Making webpages, and HTML/JS: Making webpages interactive.

Your Big Story

Welcome to a cross between Mad Libs and a fantasy novel, where each time through, the story's a little different. This app is our longest program yet, but we're ready. It uses many programming basics we've seen before, plus a new element that joins words and variables together. (It's called concatenation.)

> Get this code working, and then totally change it up and remix it into *your* vision, because code is about expressing *your* voice and ideas, and telling *your* story.

Without further ado! Our story will go something like this:

```
Welcome to Your Big Story.
What's your name?  Nitya
Hi, Nitya
Are you a president, a panda or a lovebug?
Panda
Okay, Panda. What day is today?  Friday
A thousand years back, Nitya journeyed to the
High Point. At dusk on Friday, everyone
gathered in the clearing. The happy Flora gave
Nitya her very own red royal robe. When the
northern bell chimed, they set off to climb high.
```

QUESTIONS AND ANSWERS

STORY

The code is long, so we'll divide it into 5 sections. That will make it easier to work through. Tough-road-ahead warning: there may be some teeth-gritting when it comes time to join together the variables and strings and spaces. That's okay, though; if it takes you a few times to get it right, just keep repeating to yourself, "Hard is okay. I can troubleshoot this. Hard is okay. . . ."

When you're ready, open a new Python 3 file in trinket.io and code along.

SECTION 1

In the first section, we want to:

1 Welcome the player.

2 Ask the player to enter some data:

* Her name
* A character she chooses from the list
* The day of the week

When we get each answer, we'll make some variables to store the answers in.

CODE LIKE A GIRL

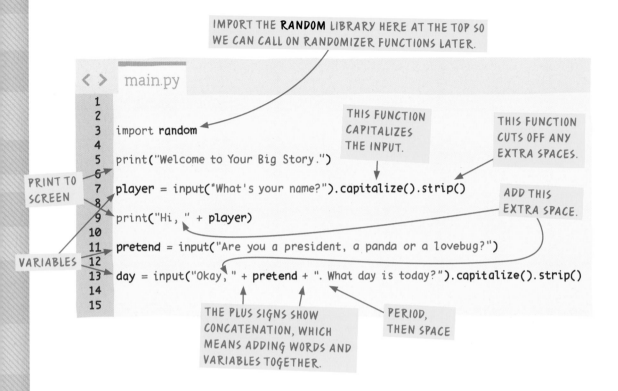

IMPORT THE **RANDOM** LIBRARY HERE AT THE TOP SO WE CAN CALL ON RANDOMIZER FUNCTIONS LATER.

main.py

```
1
2
3    import random
4
5    print("Welcome to Your Big Story.")
6
7    player = input("What's your name?").capitalize().strip()
8
9    print("Hi, " + player)
10
11   pretend = input("Are you a president, a panda or a lovebug?")
12
13   day = input("Okay, " + pretend + ". What day is today?").capitalize().strip()
14
15
```

THIS FUNCTION CAPITALIZES THE INPUT.

THIS FUNCTION CUTS OFF ANY EXTRA SPACES.

PRINT TO SCREEN

ADD THIS EXTRA SPACE.

VARIABLES

THE PLUS SIGNS SHOW CONCATENATION, WHICH MEANS ADDING WORDS AND VARIABLES TOGETHER.

PERIOD, THEN SPACE

We've done something like this before, with functions like print() and input(). I've tossed in some new ones: capitalize() switches the first letter into uppercase, and strip() removes any extra spaces from the end of the input. These functions keep the answer tidy.

Run these lines and debug until the code works. Here's my result:

```
Welcome to Your Big Story.
What's your name?   Elise
Hi, Elise
Are you a president, a panda or a
lovebug?   President
Okay, President. What day is today?
Tuesday
```

Now that introductions have been made, we've got to tell the program how to make decisions. I'll show you.

SECTION 2

Is the story really about presidents, pandas and lovebugs? Not exactly. In our tale, the hero gets a power object to use on her quest. There are 4 possibilities: a power shield, a glittering box, a lavender wand or a red royal robe. How do we decide which one she gets? Based on whether she chooses to be a president, a panda or a lovebug. In code, that means we take the pretend variable—it holds her choice—and run it through an if-else statement, aka a conditional!

The result: our hero claims her power object.

Once we change president, panda or lovebug into a power object, we'll store the result in a new variable, called powerObject.

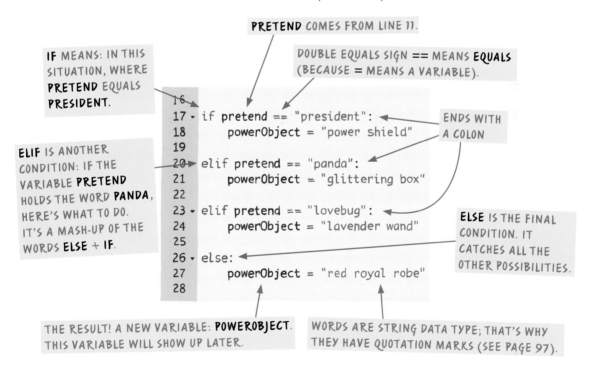

PRETEND COMES FROM LINE 11.

IF MEANS: IN THIS SITUATION, WHERE PRETEND EQUALS PRESIDENT.

DOUBLE EQUALS SIGN == MEANS EQUALS (BECAUSE = MEANS A VARIABLE).

ELIF IS ANOTHER CONDITION: IF THE VARIABLE PRETEND HOLDS THE WORD PANDA, HERE'S WHAT TO DO. IT'S A MASH-UP OF THE WORDS ELSE + IF.

ENDS WITH A COLON

ELSE IS THE FINAL CONDITION. IT CATCHES ALL THE OTHER POSSIBILITIES.

```
16
17 ▸ if pretend == "president":
18        powerObject = "power shield"
19
20 ▸ elif pretend == "panda":
21        powerObject = "glittering box"
22
23 ▸ elif pretend == "lovebug":
24        powerObject = "lavender wand"
25
26 ▸ else:
27        powerObject = "red royal robe"
28
```

THE RESULT! A NEW VARIABLE: POWEROBJECT. THIS VARIABLE WILL SHOW UP LATER.

WORDS ARE STRING DATA TYPE; THAT'S WHY THEY HAVE QUOTATION MARKS (SEE PAGE 97).

We've used this pattern before: Hold something. Change it. Give it a new variable name.

Q Why do we use the double equals sign == ?

A The single equals sign = assigns a value to a variable. It would be confusing to use the same symbol for more than one thing, so the double equals sign == means "equals."

Q Back in line 11 in our code on page 112, it looks like there are 3 choices: president, panda and lovebug. Why do lines 17–27 on page 113 have 4 conditions?

A That's for the default. Say a user types in something other than *president* or *panda* or *lovebug*? Maybe she misspells the word or uses capital letters. Anything can happen. Remember the mantra that computers are stupid? For our code to run, a user must type in exactly and precisely what the computer has been programmed to receive and respond to.

That's why the fourth condition, on lines 26–27, is the default. It's like the junk drawer in our code. We toss in every answer that doesn't exactly fit. If we didn't have this fourth section, these answers would get an error message, not a story. Now, no matter what a user types in, she'll still get a power object.

Q Really??

A Totally. Flip back to our story on page 111. Notice that on the fifth line down, someone (okay, that would be me) entered "Panda"? Now look at the second-to-last line of the story. I didn't get the panda's glittering box. Why? Check out the fifth line again. I chose my character and typed "Panda" with a capital P. That's all it took to get my Panda tossed into the "else" category, and that's why I got the red royal robe, not the glittering box like the other pandas.

SECTION 3

What's happening now? We're prepping for the randomizer that will pull different words into the story each time. That way our players can play again and again and have different experiences. Let's create 4 lists: one each for names, places, feelings and quests. Sneak peek: once these are set up, we can the run the randomizer function on each of them (in section 4), and in section 5, we'll call the random words and phrases into our story.

First things first. Add these lines to your code.

EACH LIST HOLDS ITEMS THAT THE RANDOMIZER CAN CHOOSE FROM. YOU CAN TELL THEY'RE LISTS BECAUSE THEY HAVE SQUARE BRACKETS AND HOLD MANY THINGS.

MAKE 4 LISTS.
GIVE EACH LIST A NAME.

```
29
30
31
32  nameList = ["Shanise", "Danny", "Scooter", "Michelle", "Flora", "Yossi"]
33
34  placeList = ["California", "G-town", "the High Point", "Carpenter Woods"]
35
36  feelingList = ["perplexed ", "bemused ", "surprised ", "happy ", "confused "]
37
38  questList = ["find the golden path", "bring back the missing", "climb high"]
39
```

THESE ARE STRINGS, SO USE QUOTATION MARKS!

IN **FEELINGLIST**, LEAVE AN EXTRA SPACE AFTER THE WORDS. I'LL EXPLAIN WHY ON THE NEXT PAGE.

USE A COMMA TO SEPARATE EACH STRING FROM THE NEXT. COMMAS GO <u>OUTSIDE</u> THE QUOTATION MARKS.

SECTION 4

Ready for the randomizer? These next 4 lines are powerhouses. They'll choose 1 element from each of the lists we just made.

THESE ARE RANDOM CHOICE FUNCTIONS.

```
40
41  name = random.choice(nameList)
42  place = random.choice(placeList)
43  feeling = random.choice(feelingList)
44  quest = random.choice(questList)
45
```

PASS IN THE VARIABLES FROM LINES 32–38. EACH ONE HOLDS A LIST.

STORE THE RESULT IN A NEW VARIABLE.

ALMOST THERE!

We have the building blocks for our story now, even though whatever will be picked will be a surprise to us! We can't see the work being done, but the results are stored inside each of these new variables. Coming up, we'll call up our random picks and weave them into our story, Mad Libs–style.

SECTION 5

At long last! We've been journeying through code, 4 intense sections of it. The time has come to write the parts of the story that won't change, and then reach into our variables, and let the computer take out the secret random words held inside and plug them into our story. For all of this, we use concatenation, which you can just call "joining everything together." See all the plus signs? That's concatenation. The plus signs connect the unchanging words of the story and the variables. This makes the complete story. Because the variables can hold any word or phrase that the user enters, the story changes each time.

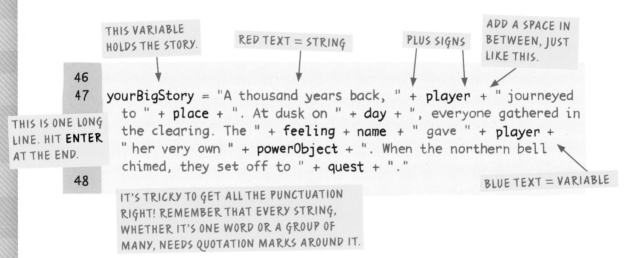

THIS VARIABLE HOLDS THE STORY.

RED TEXT = STRING

PLUS SIGNS

ADD A SPACE IN BETWEEN, JUST LIKE THIS.

THIS IS ONE LONG LINE. HIT **ENTER** AT THE END.

```
46
47   yourBigStory = "A thousand years back, " + player + " journeyed
     to " + place + ". At dusk on " + day + ", everyone gathered in
     the clearing. The " + feeling + name + " gave " + player +
     " her very own " + powerObject + ". When the northern bell
     chimed, they set off to " + quest + "."
48
```

BLUE TEXT = VARIABLE

IT'S TRICKY TO GET ALL THE PUNCTUATION RIGHT! REMEMBER THAT EVERY STRING, WHETHER IT'S ONE WORD OR A GROUP OF MANY, NEEDS QUOTATION MARKS AROUND IT.

Some tricky stuff to watch out for:

1. Python doesn't add spaces between words, so we have to code that ourselves. Run the program. If words scrunch together, go back in and add spaces where you need them, between the words of the story and the quotation marks. (That's why, on line 36 on page 115, we added a space after each word in feelingList—to make it easier here.)

2 Strings (those unchanging words that will appear in the story) have quotation marks, but variables don't. That's one way this part of the code gets a little funky. When you troubleshoot, make sure to spell the variable names correctly, and to get quotation marks in the right places—around the words and the extra spaces.

Now for the final line of code, which will print the story on your screen.

THIS VARIABLE HOLDS THE STORY.

```
49  print(yourBigStory)
```

PRINT TO SCREEN

Ready to press the Run button and see the result of all that code? Do it!

```
Welcome to Your Big Story.
What's your name?  Casey
Hi, Casey
Are you a president, a panda or a lovebug?
lovebug
Okay, lovebug. What day is today?  monday
A thousand years back, Casey journeyed to
California. At dusk on Monday, everyone
gathered in the clearing. The bemused Scooter
gave Casey her very own lavender wand. When
the northern bell chimed, they set off to
climb high.
```

If your program works the first time, amazing! If not, do what coders do: debug. It goes without saying that my program took many tries to get right. Coders troubleshoot and solve problems all day long. They search online and ask their friends for help.

When the program finally runs, there's a spirit-lifting sensation that you can create anything, climb higher and faster than anyone. That the world is yours to build. Enjoy that. And of course, once you get the program running, change it. Iterate! Add more conditions, new names and places and quests, and definitely write your own story. Always.

Dear Reader,

That was a lot. Umpteen variables. Rowdy randomizers. Piles of plus signs.

We are deep in the land of code. Turn back to the opening pages of this chapter, and even to the start of the book, so you can feel how far you've come. Now you know the 5 basic concepts of coding: loops and variables, conditionals and functions and lists. You know about data types like strings and integers. You know that a library holds extra functions, and that you can make your own functions. You even know how to join strings and variables together. With these basics, you'll be ready to learn pretty much any programming language. Each language has different commands and its own syntax, or set of rules. It may use other symbols, like $ { } || and &. But the general concepts remain the same.

Finally, a gazillion high fives from me for sticking with Python till the end. We'll use Python again in Chapter 5 to code short programs that make LEDs light up.

Take it from here, and dream up your own programs and apps, whether they're shortish, like these, or longer. Apps aren't just apps, really; they're ideas and creative possibilities that people build with code.

 LOVE, MIRIAM

P.S. MORE PYTHON

Want to code more Python? Search around on trinket.io for their tutorials and look on codelikeagirlbook.com.

CHAPTER 4

TINKERING

Dear Reader,

I met Leslie Birch on a drizzly gray Saturday morning. She had organized a workshop on Amazon's Alexa, and it began at 9 a.m. at Drexel University's ExCITe Center, which is famous for creative technology. I stopped by because a Python programmer named Becca had told me I just had to get to know Leslie.

Leslie's a tinkerer and an inventor. She's famous among makers for the FLORAbrella: a clear bubble umbrella decked out with raindrop-like LED light strips. To turn the lights into raindrops, she

FLORABRELLA

programmed an Arduino microcontroller to run the lights. Then she added a battery pack and made sure the electrical circuit was fully connected. In other words: she mixed together an electrical circuit with code. Voilà, the colorful FLORAbrella was born.

Q What's a microcontroller?

A A mini-computer that runs just one program at a time.

Leslie had taught herself how to code "skills," which are programs for Alexa, and because of that, she'd won this workshop from Amazon. She's like that; she follows her creative vision wherever it takes her. When I said hi to Leslie, I held out my hand to shake. Instead, she gave me a big, welcoming hug. "I don't even know you, but thank goodness you're here. We're just about the only women!" I looked around. It was true! The room was mostly guys. That was definitely weird, because so many women in the maker community are doing amazing things with lights and sensors, electricity, art and code.

We're going to join them. That's right. It's time for electricity and circuits, and to get started, we'll use low-voltage coin batteries and LED lights.

So what exactly is tinkering?

Tinkering is about seeing a problem and finding a solution. It doesn't have to be elegant. It's the spirit of "Hey, let's try it this way," of imagining and popping things together to get to a first draft, a possibility, a prototype.

Prototype is a big word for the first version of a great idea.

In tinkering, you might start with full directions or maybe some knowledge of the first few steps. Or not, and you're going to follow your hunch and a vision, and trust your mind and hands to figure it out.

Trusting yourself is key. Tinkering means believing that you can create what you see in your mind's eye.

So where to do all this tinkering? Some of you may have hung out at a makerspace at your school or library, a room filled with tools, supplies, batteries, wires, and maybe some laser cutters and 3-D printers and sewing machines. But a makerspace can be more casual, too, and less permanent. Today, my makerspace was my dining room table, filled with LEDs and jumper wires, because I was making a lantern. Sometimes my makerspace moves to the basement or the back shed or a desk. It's not really the space that matters, but you and your vision.

Electrical circuits are a fun way to get started with tinkering and makerspaces. These may be new to some of us, but we're going for it.

I'm so glad we've reached this point. Welcome to the adventure ahead.

 LOVE, MIRIAM

P.S. WE'LL USE THESE MATERIALS TO DO THE PROJECTS IN THIS CHAPTER.

SPECIAL SUPPLIES TO BUILD CIRCUITS

- ☐ String of micro LED lights
- ☐ LEDs—small lights
- ☐ Resistors (220, 270, or 330 ohms)
- ☐ CR2032 coin batteries (these can be relatively inexpensive when purchased in 10-packs)
- ☐ Surface-mount coin-battery holders. These attach batteries to fabric.
- ☐ Conductive thread, the softest kind you can find
- ☐ Copper tape or copper strips—or, in a pinch, aluminum foil

AROUND-THE-HOUSE STUFF AND ARTSY THINGS

- ☐ Mason jar or other glass jar with a lid
- ☐ Earbuds
- ☐ Scarf, hat, gloves or mittens and other clothing
- ☐ Embroidery floss, yarn or twine
- ☐ Paper, cardboard and card stock
- ☐ Fabric and felt, from old clothes and such
- ☐ Large picture frame (with glass)
- ☐ Needle and thread
- ☐ Metal sew-on snaps
- ☐ Clear tape and duct tape
- ☐ Glue
- ☐ Dry-erase markers, or any markers
- ☐ Binder clips
- ☐ Safety pins
- ☐ Birthday cards that sing or play music when you open them
- ☐ Old light-up shoes and light-up toys you can take apart
- ☐ Tools: scissors, screwdrivers, mini-screwdrivers, flat-nose pliers

Where do you find these special supplies? Try a site like adafruit.com or sparkfun.com, or a local craft or electronics store. This book's website has a way to purchase all of them together in a pack (go to codelikeagirlbook.com/supplies).

P.P.S. I ASKED LESLIE A FEW QUESTIONS.

Q Leslie, tell me about your Space Station pin.

A Well, about every 90 minutes, the International Space Station circles the Earth, so I made a pin that lights up when the Space Station flies overhead! It's called the NASA ISS pin, and it uses LEDs and a wireless connection to spotthestation.nasa.gov. (You can find Leslie's directions on adafruit.com and make your own.) I also made a Space Station skirt where the sensors light up the LEDs around the skirt depending on where the ISS is.

Q That's great! What's next on your vision list?

A I'm working on an art installation about storm-water runoff—you swish your hands in a water bowl, and that triggers projected images. I'm also involved in Public Lab, which is an international organization that monitors environmental issues around the world. Oh, and I have an idea about conductive icing. That's right, imagine a cake with icing that blinks!!

DIY Smartphone Glove

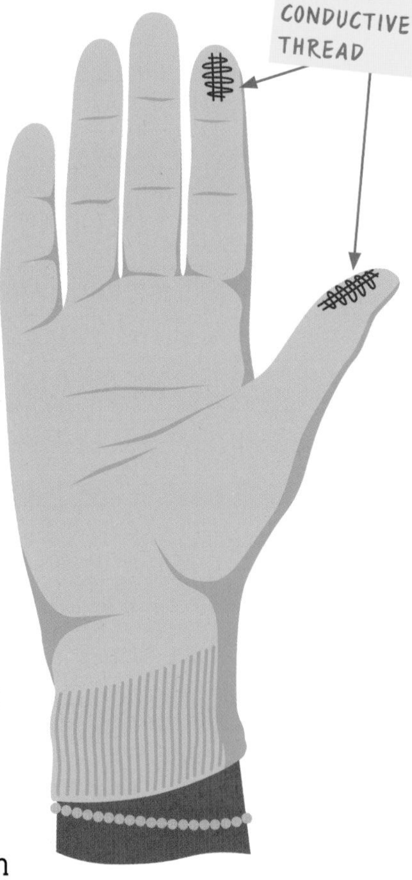
PATCH OF CONDUCTIVE THREAD

It's winter. You're waiting for the bus, or you're at a soccer game, your gloves are on and you want to use your smartphone. Maybe you're at home but there's a chill. You pull on mittens to feel cozy, but still you want to watch videos and send texts. You realize that you can turn your gloves or mittens into those expensive smartphone gloves, all by yourself and at a fraction of the cost.

How does the smartphone glove work? Phones and tablets have "capacitive" touch screens that work because your fingers conduct electricity. Whenever you touch the screen with your bare finger, a connection or circuit is created between your finger and the screen, which is programmed to react in certain ways to what it senses and to how you move your fingers.

THE CIRCUIT WORKS SOMETHING LIKE THIS:

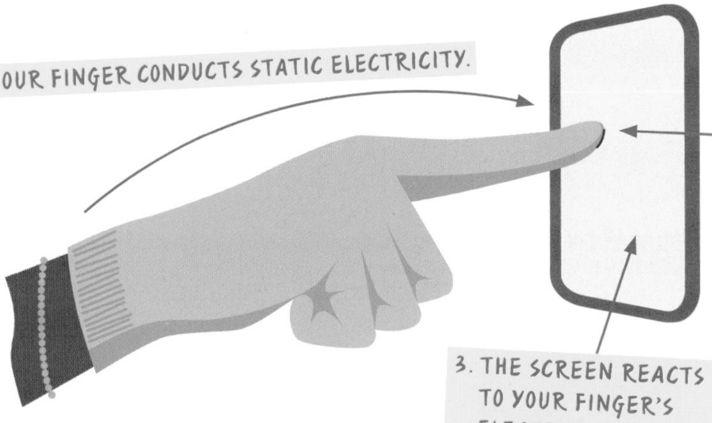
1. YOUR FINGER CONDUCTS STATIC ELECTRICITY.
2. THE THREAD PATCH CONNECTS YOUR FINGER TO THE TOUCH SCREEN.
3. THE SCREEN REACTS TO YOUR FINGER'S ELECTRICAL CHARGE.

Gloves and mittens get in the way and break that circuit, which is why you can't text while wearing them. To restore the circuit and reconnect the heat from your finger to the screen, we're going to loop in a patch of conductive thread.

MATERIALS

- ☐ Gloves or mittens
- ☐ Needle
- ☐ Conductive thread

Conductive thread is super-flexible soft wire. To find some at home: if you have broken earbuds around, strip off the covering—by hand or with a wire-stripper tool—and use the wire inside. Just make sure the wire is soft; you don't want it scratching the glass on your phone or tablet.

1. Thread the needle with the conductive thread and tie a good knot at the end.

2. Pull on the mitten or glove. Locate the exact spot on (or by) the first finger you use to control your device. The spot may be smaller than you think. Cover this spot with 5 to 7 overlapping stitches. Tie a knot and cut the thread.

3. Repeat step 2 to make a patch on the thumb.

4. Try it out. If the connection doesn't work yet, add more stitches to make a thicker connection, or move the patches to a better spot.

> You may need fewer stitches to make it work, or more. That's tinkering: doing whatever it takes to make an idea work.

CODE LIKE A GIRL

LED Light-Up Scarf

Decorate a scarf with a string of micro LEDs. An LED string is a very basic circuit. The electrical flow starts at the battery pack. A wire leaves the positive pole of the battery and stretches up through the LED string to the end, where it turns back toward the battery's negative pole. A switch on the battery pack turns the circuit on and off by interrupting the flow of electricity.

LEDS

BATTERY PACK

Q What's an LED?

A Short for light-emitting diode, an LED uses much less energy than a traditional bulb. It glows but doesn't get hot. The "diode" part of the name? In diodes, energy flows in only one direction, from positive to negative.

MATERIALS

☐ Scarf or cloth

☐ String(s) of micro LED lights

☐ Needle and thread, or duct tape, or safety pins

☐ Battery: if the LED string doesn't come with batteries, you'll probably need a CR2032 coin battery

On loosely knit scarves, you may be able to attach the string of lights to a large-eyed needle and then weave it in and through the scarf. Otherwise use safety pins to attach the LED string to the scarf, and then use a regular needle and thread to sew the LED string onto the scarf. Remove the pins after the LED string is sewn on.

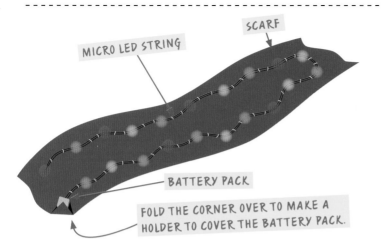

MICRO LED STRING

SCARF

BATTERY PACK

FOLD THE CORNER OVER TO MAKE A
HOLDER TO COVER THE BATTERY PACK.

Make anything light up! Add micro LED strings to outdoor
gear, clothing, fabric, glasses and jewelry.

Baseball-Cap Earbuds

MATERIALS

☐ Hat

☐ Earbuds

☐ Safety Pins

☐ Needle and thread or duct tape

Earbuds have a problem: they tangle. They just do. They're long and thin, and
their Y shape means that there are not 2 but 3 strands to coil together in a
twisty knot. See if one of these projects can fix that problem.

Start by imagining and sketching how you want to attach the earbuds to a hat.
Use whatever hat you wear: baseball cap, wool hat, beret or anything. If you
wear a headscarf, go with that. Then use safety pins to make a prototype—
that's your phase 1 attempt to make it work. The earbuds should fit along the
back of the hat so that when it's on your head, it's easy to tuck them into your
ears; just keep tinkering till you find the right position. For phase 2, use a
needle and thread, or use duct tape creatively.

Friendship Bracelet–Style Earbud Detangler

Can we hack the tangling problem by making the earbuds thicker? You could wrap duct tape around them, but that would get sticky, especially in hot weather. How about this: use some embroidery floss, thread or yarn to cover the earbud wires with a basic friendship-bracelet knot.

MATERIALS

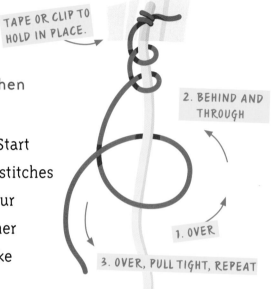

TAPE OR CLIP TO HOLD IN PLACE.

2. BEHIND AND THROUGH

1. OVER

3. OVER, PULL TIGHT, REPEAT

☐ Earbuds

☐ Embroidery floss, thread, yarn, kitchen twine or whatever you can find

1 Tie thread to the end of the earbuds. Start tying friendship knots, and push the stitches together to keep them tight. When your thread runs out, you can attach another length to it, and change colors to make whatever designs you want.

2 When you reach the point where the earbuds split into 2 wires, tie on a second thread.

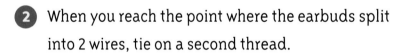

Make sure not to cover the microphone or any controls!

3 Tie several knots to finish. Tuck in or clip off the leftover thread.

Will it work? Will the earbuds never tangle again? That's the thing about tinkering and hacking. It's so incredibly optimistic. You can't predict whether it will work, and you won't know until you try.

Tech-ify Your Room with a DIY Glass Board

This isn't a circuit, but every tech and code project needs a place to brainstorm. True, you could just sketch your idea on paper, but all the tech and design companies use whiteboards and glass walls. If they get to scribble on walls, so should we.

Instead of a whiteboard (which uses a special kind of paint), we'll make a glass board. You can cover your walls with glass, of course, but that's a big expense. You can find old picture frames of all sizes at yard sales and secondhand stores, and that's what we'll use to make a glass board.

MATERIALS

☐ Large picture frame (with glass)

☐ Paper (any color)

☐ Dry-erase markers, or any markers, in any colors that will show up against the paper you use

1 Does paper cover the back of the frame? Remove it and loosen the pins around the edges, using your fingers or a screwdriver or a coin. Take the layers apart and set them aside. If the glass is dirty, clean it and let it dry, then put it back in the frame.

Watch out for sharp glass edges and pins!

129

2 Insert paper instead of a picture into the frame. This will be the backdrop. Light-colored paper makes it easier to see what you've written. Draw lines on the paper—or anything you want as the background—or just leave it blank.

3 Replace all the layers and pins on the back of the frame.

4 Use dry-erase markers to write on the glass. They are easy to erase— just use a tissue or paper towel or even an official "dry eraser." Most other markers will come off with a damp tissue.

The Tinkering Journey Continues

Circuit has the same origin as the word *circle;* it's from the Latin root *circ,* meaning "around." A circle is a connection. There are friendship circles and family circles, and even vicious circles, out of which progress cannot be made. We can run circles around something, or circle the wagons for protection. Concentric circles ripple out from each other, never to touch. We can join a support circle or a drumming circle or a literary circle. We can frustratingly go in circles, or come full circle, or find ourselves in the winner's circle.

In other words, circuits are electricity flowing in a circle.

In a working circuit, power leaves the positive side of the battery or electrical outlet. It circles through the wires and components so it can deliver electricity to them, and then returns to the power source through the negative side.

The root *circ* is also related to *circus*, for its round rings, but I'll leave it to you to make a metaphor out of that.

MAKE SHELVES TO STORE YOUR STUFF

Cardboard is a handy material to make things out of, and to prototype—or create "first tries"—for projects. Here's a tinkering project for your new makerspace: DIY shelves made from cardboard boxes. You can use smaller boxes as drawers that fit into larger boxes. Another model, shown here, bends cardboard into triangles, then uses duct tape to hold together each triangle and connect the triangles to each other.

Tech and tinkering often come down to some materials and a vision and questions: How do the boxes hold together? How can they be connected to the wall so they won't topple over? (Duct tape? Large binder clips?) Want more ideas? Search Pinterest and other sites for "cardboard box shelves," and see if those images inspire you to re-create them at home.

HERE'S ONE WAY TO DO IT: CUT AND FOLD CARDBOARD INTO TRIANGLES.

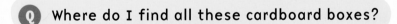

Q Where do I find all these cardboard boxes?

A Ask at local stores. Giving boxes to you means less recycling for them. If you live in an apartment building, check your trash room.

2 Now tape this to the inside of the jar's lid so the LED will stick up into the glass jar. Twist the lid back onto the jar, turn the jar upside down, and your lantern is ready.

Q Can I attach 2 LEDs to 1 battery?

A There's some math involved in circuits. An LED needs 2 to 3 volts of electricity to glow. A CR2032 coin battery has 3 volts, so 1 coin battery for 1 LED works. Two LEDs, however, need double that, or 4 to 6 volts. Since a single battery still only has 3 volts, there won't be enough voltage to go around, especially if you touch both LEDs directly to the battery. In other words, try it. The LEDs are likely to flicker and shine less brightly, because they have to share the power.

Light-Up Cards from Paper and Copper Tape

Let's kick it up a notch and make a larger circuit. In our ultra-simple circuit, the battery and LED touched. Most circuits add an on/off switch so the flow of electricity can be controlled. This twinkling light-up card uses a larger circuit made of copper tape and adds a homemade switch.

How does the on/off switch work? When you fold the flap over the battery and hold it down, the copper tape on the flap touches the top of the battery and completes the circuit. Hold everything tight. The electricity will flow—and the LED will turn on. To keep the switch in the "on" position, use a binder clip or anything you find that's strong enough to hold the battery against the copper tape so the power can flow through.

MATERIALS

- ☐ 2 LEDs
- ☐ CR2032 coin battery
- ☐ Copper tape or copper strips (in a pinch, use aluminum foil)
- ☐ Clear tape
- ☐ Card stock, cardboard or paper for the card
- ☐ Binder clip

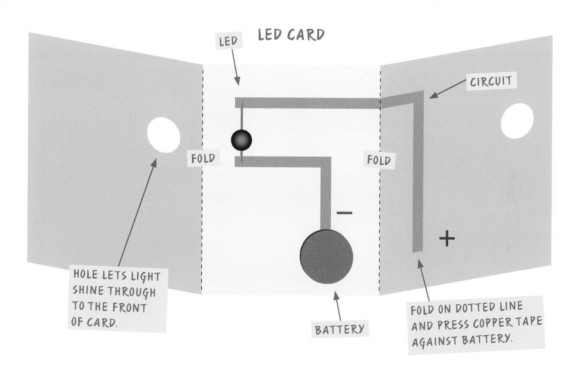

LED CARD

LED

CIRCUIT

FOLD

FOLD

HOLE LETS LIGHT SHINE THROUGH TO THE FRONT OF CARD.

−

+

BATTERY

FOLD ON DOTTED LINE AND PRESS COPPER TAPE AGAINST BATTERY.

This paper circuit can turn into nearly anything: craft projects or a costume, a school presentation with attention-grabbing lights, masks for Halloween and carnivals, light-up wood projects or LED-inspired party clothing. Instead of LED lights, for instance, you can attach a buzzer that sounds when the circuit is connected.

1   On the paper, sketch dotted lines, as shown on page 135 and below, and crease and then open.

2   Place the copper tape on the paper, as shown. The copper strips may have a sticky backing, but if not, use tape to hold them down.

3   Tape the LED legs directly to the copper strip. Make sure to follow the circuit, with the longer leg/lead connecting to the positive side and the shorter leg/lead to the negative side.

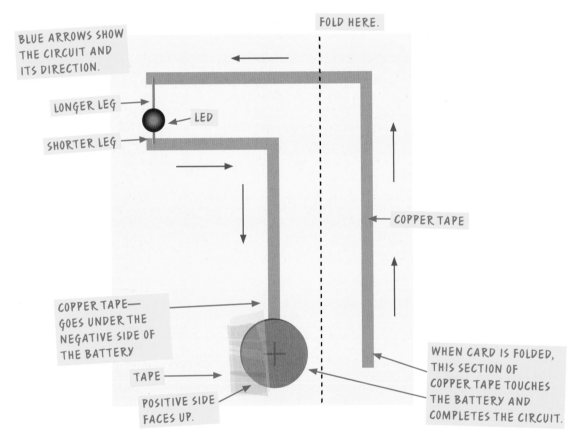

FOLD HERE.

BLUE ARROWS SHOW THE CIRCUIT AND ITS DIRECTION.

LONGER LEG

LED

SHORTER LEG

COPPER TAPE

COPPER TAPE— GOES UNDER THE NEGATIVE SIDE OF THE BATTERY

TAPE

POSITIVE SIDE FACES UP.

WHEN CARD IS FOLDED, THIS SECTION OF COPPER TAPE TOUCHES THE BATTERY AND COMPLETES THE CIRCUIT.

4   Place the battery negative side down, and lay it on top of the copper strip, as shown. Tape down the battery to attach it firmly to the copper strip, making sure the tape covers only *half* of the battery. **You want to leave exposed space on the battery so it can directly touch the other piece of copper tape,** the one that will fold over to close the circuit and allow the electricity to flow. That's it! You finished the circuit.

5 Close the card and complete the circuit. (Make sure that copper tape doesn't touch other copper tape. The height of the battery should prevent this.) When you get the circuit working, draw a circle on the part of the front of the card that's directly over the battery. Label this ("Press here" or something like that!) so it's clear where someone should press to turn the card on. Cut a small hole in both side panels to let the LED poke through. Fix up any last things with the circuit, and add words and design.

Q Mine doesn't work.

A No problem. Just as in coding, debugging is a big part of making circuits. Retrace your steps. Imagine how the electricity flows and then figure out where the circuit is breaking. Jiggle things around. Tape the LED legs so they connect 100% with the copper tape. Double-check how the copper tape turns the corner. Make sure the copper tape doesn't fold over onto itself. Touch the battery and LED together to make sure both are working.

I Want More Light and Color!

It's limiting, working with only 1 LED! You can add more LEDs by using a parallel circuit. In this type of circuit, the LEDs will share the battery power among themselves.

Remember the micro LED string we used to make a light-up scarf? That was a parallel circuit that shared the battery power among all the lights. We'll use the same design here for 2 LEDs. Start with the illustration on page 136. Then tape down the legs of a second LED, as in the top right illustration on page 138, with the longer one touching the copper tape/positive flow and the shorter touching the negative direction, just like the first LED. Then poke another hole through the front of the card so we can see the second LED.

4 Sew! With the conductive thread and a needle, sew from the battery holder's positive side to the positive side of the LED and tie a knot around the spiral. When you're done, cut the thread. Now tie a knot around the square, negative side and sew toward the snap. When you arrive at the snap, use many stitches to connect it to the fabric tightly. Tie off the thread and cut it. Now attach the thread to the second snap, sew it tightly to the bracelet with lots of stitches and then sew till you're back at the battery holder's negative side. Connect the thread to the battery holder—you'll see where—and tie it off and cut. That's it. You just hand-made your circuit.

> The goal: super-strong connections all along the circuit, with no floppiness. Sew small stitches and pull them tight.

5 Hey, your circuit is done. Click the battery into the holder. Usually the negative side faces down and lies on top of the "negative" clips. A second pair of clips will touch the top, or positive side.

SECRETS OF THE COIN-BATTERY HOLDER

By now you've realized that every part of tech is a problem to solve! Here's how the battery holder works.

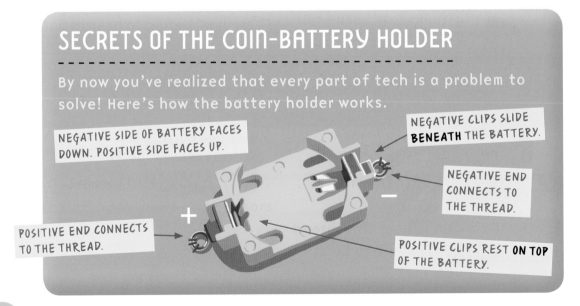

NEGATIVE SIDE OF BATTERY FACES DOWN. POSITIVE SIDE FACES UP.

NEGATIVE CLIPS SLIDE **BENEATH** THE BATTERY.

NEGATIVE END CONNECTS TO THE THREAD.

POSITIVE END CONNECTS TO THE THREAD.

POSITIVE CLIPS REST **ON TOP** OF THE BATTERY.

6 To test the circuit, close the snaps. I hope your bracelet lights up the first time, but you know how it goes with technology: that would be a miracle! Troubleshoot and debug until it works.

7 Once the miracle happens and the LED works, cut a second piece of fabric or felt to wrap around the first. Use a needle and regular thread (not conductive), or glue, or anything you want, to attach the 2 long sides. This wrapper covers the battery and keeps the conductive thread away from your skin. It's not a lot of current, but we want to be doubly safe—AND who wants the circuit to show? Cut a hole in this wrapper so the LED can peek out. Leave the snaps showing.

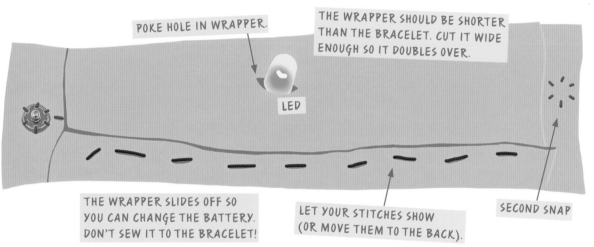

POKE HOLE IN WRAPPER.

THE WRAPPER SHOULD BE SHORTER THAN THE BRACELET. CUT IT WIDE ENOUGH SO IT DOUBLES OVER.

LED

THE WRAPPER SLIDES OFF SO YOU CAN CHANGE THE BATTERY. DON'T SEW IT TO THE BRACELET!

LET YOUR STITCHES SHOW (OR MOVE THEM TO THE BACK).

SECOND SNAP

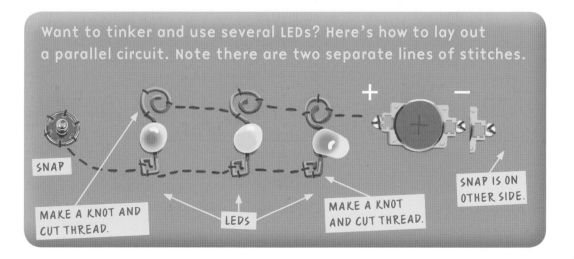

Want to tinker and use several LEDs? Here's how to lay out a parallel circuit. Note there are two separate lines of stitches.

SNAP

MAKE A KNOT AND CUT THREAD.

LEDS

MAKE A KNOT AND CUT THREAD.

SNAP IS ON OTHER SIDE.

Two Big Words, *Prototype* and *Iteration* (aka First Tries and Continuous Tinkering)

Once you've had that "aha" moment with circuits, you can make nearly anything. The process? Imagine. Have an idea. Then sketch it, whether it's a light-up game, poster, bracelet, hat, jacket or costume. Think about the materials you need, and gather them. You're on the way to making your prototype, which is the early version of how your idea will work. Even a first-round prototype goes through many iterations, or versions; small shifts and turns are at the core of tinkering. After all, these aren't ready-made projects that come in a box; they are your new and creative visions. So in the spirit of anti-perfectionism: tinker, tinker and tinker.

This, in a nutshell, is how any tech product designer works: She starts with a vision—and she experiments—and she builds a prototype—and tests it out—and experiments more—and asks others for tons of feedback—and tinkers some more . . . until the magic happens! Then, when the prototype is truly ready, she—and you—will figure out how to move your invention into production, and then to market, so real people can use it. That's how a vision becomes a reality and changes lives.

Take Things Apart

Tinkering is about putting things together *and* taking them apart, too. It can feel quite freeing and powerful to peer inside electronics. Take apart light-up toys, an old phone or the leftover remote control from a long-gone TV.

Definitely unplug electronics before taking them apart!

Pull apart an old computer keyboard, and you may be amazed to find a rubber dome. Beneath that you may find a beautiful matrix board that looks like pathways through a garden. A keyboard is like a mini-computer. Here's how it works: When you press a key, it completes the circuit in a specific place. The keyboard's microcontroller interprets the changes in electrical flow that result when you type, and translates that change into a W, g, $, @ or #—or whatever key you pressed—and sends that info to the computer.

MICROCONTROLLER

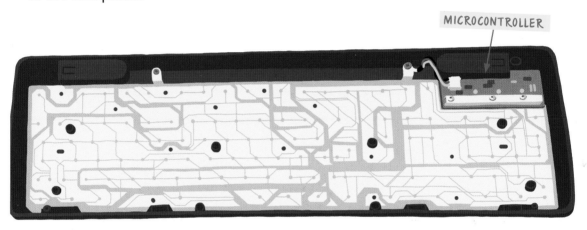

Use mini-screwdrivers to remove the small screws that hold together many toys and electronics.

Circling Back to Code

Let me tell you the story of where we're headed. Everything electronic in your life works because a circuit of electricity either flows or stops. Computing works because way down beneath all the layers of code, there's an electrical signal that's either on or off. That's it. All our code translates to this. Music apps, video apps, Snapchat, Instagram, and all the apps that haven't been created yet: in the end, they compile and translate into a series of electrical signals that are either on or off. That's right, at base, every command eventually turns into groupings of 1's and 0's, which stand for on and off. I know, it's crazy but true. Code is actually about electricity!

So what's next on our tech adventure? We've got electrical circuits, so we can add power. We've got LED lights. Now we're going to add code to our circuits. First stop, though: let's take some things apart to see how they work.

Light-Up Sneakers

I put out word that I was looking for toddler light-up sneakers, the kind that kids jump up and down in to make twinkle. I won't name the mom who responded, lest her daughter read this book in 10 years, realize "*That's where my favorite worn-out, too-small sneakers went*" and get really mad. You totally don't have to admit you ever wore or even wanted light-ups, but if you spot a leftover pair at your house or a nearby thrift shop or yard sale, take one apart along with me.

After snatching light-up sneakers from this unsuspecting neighborhood child, I pulled out the removable sole and cut away layer after layer. (Ask an adult for help; sneakers are actually pretty tough, and I used tin snips, which look like oversized scissors.) After clipping the sides and then the bottom, I found the controller! It was wedged into a plastic grid inside the sole of the shoe. What's it look like?

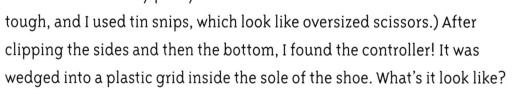

It's a 1-inch-square green circuit board that's encased in clear epoxy, which is a kind of plastic. The circuit board connects to 6 wires, which divide into 3 positive/negative pairs. Follow each pair of wires to their very end and you'll see a tiny LED.

This circuit creates the magic of a light-up shoe.

WHO KNEW?!

The device had a sticker with a web address and a product number. I was soon on the website, relieved to find the Chinese translated into English. There was no way to get inside the controller, and that's by design. It has to withstand a ton of wear and tear from active kids dancing around to make their shoes light up.

How does the circuit work? Inside the plastic is a vibration sensor. When triggered by movement, it will touch the battery, and this motion closes the circuit. The electricity then flows, which sends a signal that makes the LEDs flash for 4 beats, then double-time for 4 more beats. That's programmed in.

Can you think of a way to reuse one of these? Imagine: a friend taps you on the arm, and because you've attached the sensor to your jacket, the lights that you've sewn in start to twinkle!

Musical Birthday Cards

You know those musical birthday cards that play a song when opened? Let's take one apart. Open the card—the music will play—and now peel away the paper that covers the mechanism inside. Likely, you'll see something like this:

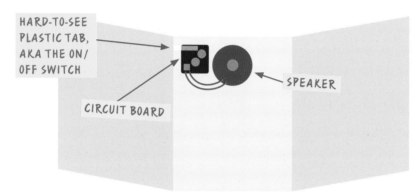

HARD-TO-SEE PLASTIC TAB, AKA THE ON/OFF SWITCH

CIRCUIT BOARD

SPEAKER

What's going on? When the card is closed, a plastic tab about an inch long slides to break the circuit and stop the power flow. Open the card and the plastic tab pulls away. Now the power can move through the circuit. The electricity flows and activates the microcontroller, which has a chip that sends a digital signal to the speaker, and the song plays. Close the card and the plastic tab will once again interrupt all this action, and the music will stop.

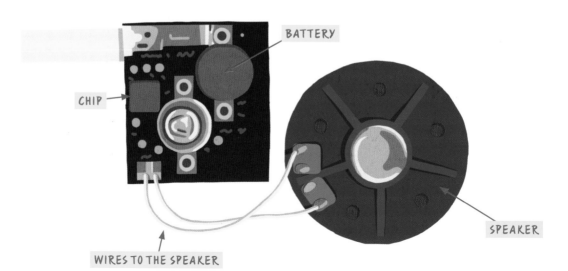

BATTERY

CHIP

SPEAKER

WIRES TO THE SPEAKER

Remember Those Light-Up Animal Pillows . . .

Do you remember these? They were all the rage: plushy animals with lights on the inside that projected stars on your ceiling? In our house it was a soft, plushy stuffed dog. On the belly, there was a plastic cover with cutout stars and a puppy's face. If you flipped the power switch on, a blue light shone through the cutouts. In the dark, this would project a puppy's face and a sea of blue stars onto the ceiling for 20 seconds. Then the light turned red, and red stars filled the ceiling for another 20 seconds, followed by green stars, and back to blue, and on and on. You get the idea; the cute pillow is an in-house light show.

So let's take it apart. Mine popped open with just a few twists of a screwdriver. Tucked inside was a plastic basket with a circuit board and 3 LEDs, along with a tiny silicon chip that holds the code that tells the LEDs what to do. There's also a battery and an on/off switch, and wires that connect all the parts. In other words, it's a pretty basic and very common electrical circuit.

I know. You'll never see LEDs in stuffed animals the same again.

CIRCUIT BOARD

ON/OFF SWITCH

BATTERY

THIS IS THE OTHER SIDE
OF THE CIRCUIT BOARD.
THESE ARE THE 3 LEDS.

And now, we can see how code mixes with circuits. Someone had to write the code and load it onto the chip and integrate it into the circuit! We can see the outside of the circuit, but we have to imagine the code inside. Programmers often use pseudo-code to express what their code should be. Pseudo-code mixes an actual coding language with English—or whatever your language is. Here, we'll spin up an English-Python mix that shows what the light-up pet code is up to.

PYTHON-ENGLISH PSEUDO-CODE

```
1
2    Import the timer
3
4 ▾ Define the LightSequence function:
5        Loop through this sequence for 20 minutes
6 ▾         For seconds 1-20:
7              Turn the blue light on
8 ▾         For seconds 21-40:
9              Turn the blue light off
10             Turn the red light on
11         For seconds 41-60:
12             Turn the red light off
13             Turn the green light on
14   Run LightSequence
15
```

In other words: Import a timer. Light each color LED alternately for 20 seconds. Keep this sequence going for 20 minutes. When 20 minutes pass, turn the power off.

In the next chapter, I'll show you how to turn pseudo-code into actual code.

Dear Reader,

"**D**on't quit." That's what Nayona told me. We were at a Girl Develop It class, and she was the teaching assistant. The room we were in had streaming sunlight and inspirational phrases on the walls, like DREAM and BE A FOUNDER and EXPERIMENT. FAIL. LEARN. REPEAT.

Nonetheless, my tech journey had hit some bumps. No one's born knowing how to code and create circuits. A million times over, I wanted to walk away. Sometimes I'd barely understand a topic. I couldn't make circuits work for the longest time. But then one night, my circuits were making LEDs flash and buzzers buzz, and I turned a light sensor into a night-light. I learned again and again to stay the course, to persist.

Keep going, because that's how you get the tech-magic reward. When that happens, you feel creative and powerful.

What's ahead in the final stop of our journey?

We just took apart cards and toys and shoes. Inside each was a circuit board. Coming up, we're going to make our own: we'll use a special DIY breadboard to make circuits and link them to Python code we write on our Raspberry Pi computers.

In case this is way outside your comfort zone, let me tell you, it was for me, too, and now I love it. The worst that can happen is that your LEDs won't light up on the first try. We can live with that. I'll explain each step as we go along. This is going to be amazing.

 LOVE, MIRIAM

CHAPTER 5

BUILD TINKER HACK CODE

Dear Reader,

I've always liked the feeling that comes with pulling everything together. If this were a novel, around this time we'd be reaching the climax and finally seeing how all the characters and places and plotline fit. Code is about telling your story, right? Our story now: We've seen what code plus circuits can do, and we're stepping into the final leg of our journey. Our adventure into tinkering continues, and we'll add code with Python.

This is true superhero stuff.

We definitely need our Raspberry Pi computer, because it has special pins that let us send code outside of a computer. We'll use jumper wires to connect the pins to a breadboard—which is a plastic-and-metal device that's perfect for trying out circuits. Then we'll code some programs that tell lights and a motion sensor what to do.

Near the end, you and I will write code that sends you an email whenever your motion sensor detects someone near your room. In other words, we'll mix code and circuits and the Internet and communication. I'm serious. Your code will send you an email. Automatically. Like the printer in my office, which auto-contacts the ink company when I'm running low, so they can send me a new supply.

I'll explain "Why?" as we go along.

We probably need a "this is awesome, but maybe hard" alert. We're not just coding. We're not just setting up a computer. We're doing both, and more—and there are lots of moving parts. You got this, though. Just take it a step at a time. Code plus circuits is the cutting edge of tech. From here, you're just a step away from making your own robots, programming your own drones or creating the best motion-activated Halloween tricks ever.

Remember that grand feeling that comes over you when it works.

Hold on tight!

 LOVE, MIRIAM

P.S. Even if you don't have a Raspberry Pi computer, keep reading. I found a way for you to do this, too.

P.P.S. Tech changes all the time. If a project doesn't work, check codelikagirlbook.com/issues.

☐ Resistors: These slow down a circuit's energy flow. Some resistors come with the LEDs, or the LED package will tell you what kind of resistor it needs.

RESISTORS

☐ Female-to-male and male-to-male jumper wires: to connect the pins on the Raspberry Pi computer to the breadboard

The 2 types of jumper wires we need are called "female-to-male" and "male-to-male." Just as with cables and plugs, people have given gender names to jumper wires. We can also call these wires innie-to-outie and outie-to-outie.

INNIE-TO-OUTIE JUMPER WIRES

OUTIE-TO-OUTIE JUMPER WIRES

Blink

Blink is the "Hello World!"/"Look Out World, Here We Come!" program for breadboards and LEDs. Here's the plan. We write the short code first, using Python. Then, on a breadboard, we build a jumper-wire circuit that connects to the pins on the Raspberry Pi computer. The code sends electricity through the pins to the LEDs and makes them blink.

MATERIALS

☐ The Raspberry Pi computer you made in Chapter 2 and the Python 3 (IDLE) text editor

☐ 1 breadboard

☐ 2 innie-to-outie (aka female-to-male) jumper wires

☐ 1 resistor (220, 270, or 330 ohms)

☐ 1 LED

ONE MORE MYSTERY: WHERE DO WE WRITE THE CODE, AND WHAT'S "IDLE"?

The Raspberry Pi computer has a special place to write and run Python 3, called IDLE.

1. Go to Menu > Programming > Python 3 (IDLE).

2. IDLE has 2 windows: the Editor, where we write programs, and the Shell window, where programs run. To test how the windows work together, let's code a "Hello World!"

3. Click on Python 3 (IDLE), and the Shell window will open. Now we need to open an Editor window: in the nav bar, click File > New File.

4. Guess what? The Editor window should open. We'll write code here. Type out: print("Hello World!").

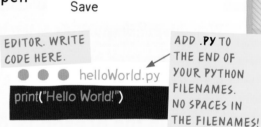

EDITOR. WRITE CODE HERE.

ADD .PY TO THE END OF YOUR PYTHON FILENAMES. NO SPACES IN THE FILENAMES!

helloWorld.py

print("Hello World!")

5. Click on File > Save. Name the file helloWorld.py and press Enter.

6. Click on Run > Run Module. Look at the Shell. Your code will run. Hello World!

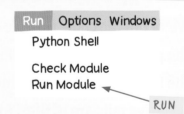

Run   Options Windows
Python Shell
Check Module
Run Module ← RUN

Python 3.7.2 Shell   Shell.

=============== helloWorld.py ===============
Hello World!
>>>

THE CODE RUNS HERE.

detects someone nearby, it will send you an email alert. Whether you're at school, at orchestra, swimming, bouncing on the trampoline, doing homework, spacing out, dreaming or hanging with your friends, you'll know when someone's invaded your room (even if it's your dog or cat).

> For this to work, you'll need a Gmail account (ask a parent or guardian if you don't have one) and you'll need to make sure your Raspberry Pi computer is connected to the Internet. (For a reminder about how, look back at Chapter 2.)

This is going to be great.

MATERIALS

If you've done the other projects, you have everything you need.
☐ Your Raspberry Pi computer and the Python 3 (IDLE) text editor
☐ 3 innie-to-innie (aka female-to-female) jumper wires
☐ 1 breadboard
☐ 1 PIR motion sensor

STEP 1

Code

Open a new Editor window in Menu › Programming › Python3 (IDLE), and start typing in the following lines of code. As you type, see what you recognize. This program works because many years ago, developers created a library called SMTP, or Simple Mail Transfer Protocol. We'll use it—and save ourselves from writing hundreds of lines of code. The result? The alert email will shoot through the Internet and into your inbox. Code is amazing, I tell you.

Remember to save! **File > Save**, and name it **emailSend.py**, or anything you'd like, with **.py** at the end.

IMPORT LIBRARIES.

```
from gpiozero import MotionSensor
from time import sleep
import smtplib
```

DEFINE THE EMAIL SEND FUNCTION.

TYPE YOUR EMAIL HERE.

```
def emailSend():
    senderEmail = "yourEmail@gmail.com"

    password = "yourPassword"

    receiverEmail = "yourEmail@gmail.com"

    message = "Subject: Someone's in your room!"

    server = smtplib.SMTP("smtp.gmail.com", 587)

    server.starttls()

    server.ehlo()

    server.login(senderEmail, password)

    server.sendmail(senderEmail, receiverEmail, message)

    server.quit()

    print ("Email Sent")
```

THESE VARIABLES HOLD INFORMATION.

CAN BE YOUR EMAIL OR SOMEONE ELSE'S.

GET ALL THE PUNCTUATION!

THESE LINES SEND OUR DATA TO THE INTERNET.

USE THE VARIABLES HERE.

```
while True:
    if MotionSensor (4).motion_detected:
        emailSend()
        print ("Who goes there?")
        sleep(2)
    else:
        print ("All quiet")
        sleep(2)
```

LOOP

TAKES IN DATA FROM THE SENSOR

IF THERE'S MOTION, LET'S USE OUR FUNCTION!

CONDITIONAL

IF NO MOTION, THEN DO THIS.

GIRL TECH WORLD

Dear Reader,

Our journey together is about to end, but yours is just beginning. You've got the tools. Lots of basic coding concepts that you'll find in any language. The Formula. Maybe you have your own Raspberry Pi computer by now. You've experienced the glories of tinkering, and can fearlessly try anything! You know to search online to find what you need.

You know more than you think you do.

So go chart your own path. Express yourself. Tell your story and build your ideas and be you, with tech and code.

WONDERING HOW TO GET STARTED WITH YOUR OWN PROJECT?

It starts with your idea—and your confidence in your vision. Sketch your idea. Break it into small pieces that you can code. Figure out the equipment you need—and the language you want to use. Google all your questions and always ask for help. Get friends involved. Keep testing and tinkering until your idea comes to life and you feel the magic.

Good luck!

I know, there's that final question lots of people have:

What About the Bro-grammer/Guys-in-Hoodies Stereotype? AKA Why Do Some People Think Tech Is a Guy Thing?

Oh yeah, that. Story first, and then some practical tips. Tech didn't always match the stereotype of guys in T-shirts and old hoodies. In fact, at the beginning, the word *computer* literally meant "females who figured out math problems really fast." Women were hired to be mathematical "computers," and from that, they began programming.

Back during World War II, the U.S. military was fighting to save the world from fascism. They needed people to do the math for how guns shoot, their range, and what kind of targets they can hit. They hired women to do that math, while a few rooms over, men worked furiously to build a computer that could calculate even faster. When that computer was finally built, the men who created it were stymied. They didn't actually know how to program the darn thing. Imagine: their ENIAC computer filled an entire room and it was noisy, and none of the guys could figure out what to do next.

CODE LIKE A GIRL

Code with Friends

Look for others who like to code. If your school has programs, sign up even if you and your friend are the only girls. You can lead the way and change this! Same with after-school and weekend programs. Have code parties and slumber parties, like hackathons. Code your way and make it fun.

> ### HOST YOUR FRIENDS FOR A SLUMBER-PARTY HACKATHON
>
> Want to get going on a weekend tech project? Call your friends. Grab some computers and tablets and phones. Set up the sleeping bags and blow-up mattresses, and stay together till you finish.

The other day I popped into an actual guy-dominated tech event, and I thought about all of you. After all, I'm a grown woman, and it was odd and awkward even for me. The weirdness lasted for the first 5 minutes. Then I decided to claim my place in the room. I decided I belonged there.

That experience made me think about what you need to know as you claim your place in tech.

1. **The dudes are not all against you.** No way, so don't go there. Some tech guys are shy. Some have undeveloped social skills. Some are just lovely and more social than the most outgoing, fun-loving girl at school. I met one tech guy who told me the first minute we met that he was really introverted and nervous around people, but he turned out to be super-social and was soon friends with everyone

184

in the room. He even left our event early because he had plans to meet up with *other* friends. Over the next few months, he generously explained lots of programming concepts to me and to others.

Whether you are 12 or 15, 25 or 50, find the good guys and hang with them. **Many people actually want more girls in tech. They want the tech world to be inclusive, and they'll go out of their way to be helpful and welcoming. Trust this, and you'll find it.**

2 **Be courageous and brave.** Any of us can be a minority in any room. Don't let the fact that you're a minority of any kind stop you. You belong.

3 **If you can make it past the first 5 minutes of shy awkwardness, you're good.** It may feel horribly weird at first, and that's okay. I tell this to myself. I tell it to my daughters. I tell it to their friends. Remember this and plan for it. What you're feeling is called discomfort, and if you can hold on, it will pass.

I know. Think of it as parameters are the possibility, and arguments are the actuality.

peanut butter and jelly sandwich A way to understand how several tiny actions make up what we think of as a single action. See page 49.

perfectionism Sounds good, but it's not. Better to goof up, make things right and move on with life. Same with code.

positive flow In a current like the ones we used, electricity flows from the positive pole to the negative one. See *negative flow* and *circuit*.

positive leg or lead On an LED, the longer leg or lead must face the positive flow of electricity.

programming One name for what we do with code. Also called developing, coding or software engineering.

prototype An early model of a project, as you start to figure things out. As in, "I prototyped my sound and light show on the breadboard. Now I'm ready to get it manufactured."

Python A general-purpose computing language with many libraries. The manual's at python.org, and to learn more, check out the resource page at djangogirls.org.

randomizer Code that picks a random number or element.

Raspberry Pi computer A computer that fits in the palm of your hand and that you can put together by yourself. Tons of tutorials, project ideas and help at raspberrypi.org. Enjoy the journey!

resistor A device that slows the flow of electricity so the LED and other components don't burn out. Readers, when it comes to resistors, I have simplified. Resistors get complicated very, very fast, with equations like Ohm's law for matching the right resistor with the electrical power flowing through the circuit.

RTFM Stands for "Read the frigging manual." Where you find all the functions and syntax for a language. What developers say to those asking questions that can be answered by reading the manual.

Scratch A programming language that uses visual blocks to build code. It is available for free at scratch.mit.edu.

sequencing Putting the steps of a program in logical order. See *The Formula.*

series circuit Electrical current flows through each LED or component, as if along a path, with the first components taking what they need and the rest getting what's left over.

solder Metal so hot it becomes liquid and holds together components in a circuit.

sprite and costume In Scratch, and in animation, a sprite is an image that can move independently. *Costume* refers to the range of looks, positions and designs that a single sprite can have.

stage In Scratch, the box that shows the results of our code.

string A data type composed (usually) of words. Numbers can be strings, but when they are, you can't do math on them.

sudo In Terminal, the owner of the account. You may have to type *sudo* before certain commands, for security. Stands for superuser do.

surface-mount coin-battery holder See *coin-battery holder.*

syntax Like English and other spoken languages, coding languages share basic elements, but each has a unique vocabulary and grammar. Think of it as the rules for coding functions, variables, loops, conditionals and more.

Terminal An awesome semi-secret place where you can control your computer, load software, move files around and find Easter eggs.

tinkering An experimental way to make projects and solve problems; you don't need to know the answer in advance. Trust yourself to create—to have an idea and make it real—and to figure things out step by step.

trinket.io Our place for writing and running code in Python, in Chapter 3, and using the Sense HAT, in Chapter 5. Check out tutorials for Python and other languages.

variable A holding space in memory where you can store a single item. You make up the name using snake_case_with_underscores, or camelCaseWithCapitalsLikeThis!

webscraping One way to collect information so you can reuse it in your app, like Fandango does for movies. Developers also use APIs (application programming interfaces) to gather data.

Acknowledgments

The best thing about writing a book? The people who become your teachers and friends. So many people are working to make tech a more inclusive and diverse and vibrant place to create with code. Here are just a few of you:

Meredith Broussard of New York University's Arthur L. Carter Journalism Institute read chapters, corrected me, hosted me in New York and re-explained the difference between methods and functions at any time, day or night. Any mistakes that remain are, sadly, mine.

Ellen Fishman, Chair of Arts and New Media at Springside Chestnut Hill Academy, is one of my #learningheroes. She brought me to my first hackathon and introduced me to Drexel University's ExCITe Center. Also at Springside Chestnut Hill: an enormous round of appreciation for Vince Day, Ed Glassman, Karen Kolkka, David Cool, Pete DiDonato, Saburah Posner, the entire Sands Center for Entrepreneurial Leadership, and to Priscilla Sands for her vision. At Drexel's ExCITe Center: Youngmoo Kim, and Kara Lindstrom as well as Andrea Forte, Thomas Park and the entire Snowball team.

Rebecca Benarroch and the girls (and boys) who braved my coding classes at Wissahickon Charter School: I am grateful for the chance to teach you and learn (even more) from you.

The Philadelphia women in tech community, especially Becca Nock, Elise Wei, Tracy Levesque, LeeAnn Kinney, Anna Lavender, Jen Dionisio, Meghan Kelly and my co-inspirations in coding: Shanise Barona, Angela Andrews, Elizabeth Hall and Nayonna Church-Purnell.

Code for Philly, the whole crew, and civic hackers everywhere. Patrick Wood, for asking me to write about my hackathon experience, and Technical.ly for printing the result. Special appreciation for everything I learned about code and design from my NearGreen hackathon team, especially Marissa Goldberg and Brad Steinberg: you never know where an app will take you.

Flatiron School, and their Women Take Tech Scholarship, for helping me learn to code.

Liz Brown, Jedi Weller and the team at webjunto.com: for inspiration, showing everyone what tech imagination, creativity and diversity look like, and allowing me to use their photo on page 6.

Jennifer Torre and Shannon Feck, formerly at Tonic Design Co., for their vision in building GRIT: Girls Rock In Tech.

Humble thank-yous to the Scratch team at MIT Media Lab; the Raspberry Pi Foundation; Sam Aaron at Sonic Pi; trinket.io; and fritzing.org: you've created awesome things for the world and you've allowed me to use your images in this book.

There's more. At TechGirlz, Tracey Welson-Rossman and Danica Pascavage; Stacey DeBroff, actualizer extraordinaire, who took me to CES; Sara Chipps, CEO of Jewelbots; Leslie Birch, maker-with-the-mostest; Georgia Guthrie at The Hacktory; John Keefe of WNYC, now at *Quartz*, and his daughters; Andruid Kerne of the Texas A&M Interface Ecology Lab; Allison Esposito and

CODE LIKE A GIRL

the Tech Ladies community; Matt Richardson at Raspberry Pi Foundation; Elliott Hauser at trinket.io; Esterling Accime; Brad Flaugher; Brad Derstine; Rachel Marcus; and my chiropractor Damien, because coding and writing for days on end can be unexpectedly tough on one's body. Laura Levitt; Jean O'Barr; Jude Ray; Dian and the Cowgirls; the High Point baristas and the morning dogwalkers of Carpenter's Woods.

Sarah Hurwitz and the Obama White House's "Helping Our Children Explore, Learn, and Dream Without Limits: Breaking Down Gender Stereotypes in Media and Toys" conference. This book began there.

My editor, Michelle Frey; assistant editor Marisa DiNovis; designers Maria Middleton, Larsson McSwain and Katrina Damkoehler; copy editors Artie Bennett and Nancee Adams and the entire editorial village at Knopf Books for Young Readers that helped create these pages. Special thanks to the amazing illustrator and designer, Sara Corbett, for her creativity and eye for detail. Much appreciation goes to Annie Suter and Kenny Taylor for test-driving the projects in the book. This book was a team effort, and I could not have done it without each of you.

Kim Schefler, my agent, first reader and first encourager.

Finally, immense gratitude to those I share daily life with: Rob, Samira and Amelia Baird. The dogs: Wiggles, the rescued pit bull who snored next to me while I wrote, and Vance, RIP, the crazy beagle who was the inspiration for Blue Dog. And of course, to Myra Peskowitz, my mom.

ABOUT THE AUTHOR

A few years ago, Miriam Peskowitz was at a White House conference on girls and technology, and wondered: "Everything's about technology and code, but who among us knows how to *create things with code*, and why is it mostly guys coding, anyway?" She'd co-written the *New York Times* and internationally bestselling *The Daring Book for Girls* and its *Double-Daring* follow-up. And she'd done some story writing for LEGO Friends. She'd landed herself at the White House to hear people from around the nation talk about why there weren't enough girls who knew how to code. But she didn't know how to code, either. That's when she began to teach herself, with workshops and classes and hackathons; she even signed up for a coding boot camp. And if she can learn to code, so can you.

Author of many books about women and girls, including *The Truth Behind the Mommy Wars*, Miriam holds a PhD from Duke University. She has been a historian, a professor of women's studies and religion, a communications and content strategist, an entrepreneur, and an investigator of all curiosities. And now . . . a coder. And she wants to make you one, too! Miriam lives in Philadelphia with her family. Find out more at codelikeagirlbook.com.

Index

cLick!

girl

DEBUG!

LANGUAGE